Counselling Children with
Special Needs

Counselling Children with Special Needs

Gill Brearley

MCSP, Cert.Ed, Dip.Counselling

Blackwell
Science

© 1997 by
Blackwell Science Ltd
Editorial Offices:
Osney Mead, Oxford OX2 0EL
25 John Street, London WC1N 2BL
23 Ainslie Place, Edinburgh EH3 6AJ
350 Main Street, Malden
  MA 02148 5018, USA
54 University Street, Carlton
  Victoria 3053, Australia

Other Editorial Offices:

Blackwell Wissenschafts-Verlag GmbH
Kurfürstendamm 57
10707 Berlin, Germany

Blackwell Science KK
MG Kodenmacho Building
7–10 Kodenmacho Nihombashi
Chuo-ku, Tokyo 104, Japan

First published 1997

Set in 10.5/13.5 pt Sabon
by DP Photosetting, Aylesbury, Bucks
Printed and bound in Great Britain by
Hartnolls Ltd, Bodmin, Cornwall

The Blackwell Science logo is a trade mark of
Blackwell Science Ltd, registered at the United
Kingdom Trade Marks Registry

DISTRIBUTORS

Marston Book Services Ltd
PO Box 269
Abingdon
Oxon OX14 4YN
(*Orders:* Tel: 01235 465500
          Fax: 01235 465555)

USA
Blackwell Science, Inc.
Commerce Place
350 Main Street
Malden, MA 02148 5018
(*Orders:* Tel: 800 759 6102
                617 388 8250
          Fax: 617 388 8255)

Canada
Copp Clark Professional
200 Adelaide Street West, 3rd Floor
Toronto, Ontario M5H 1W7
(*Orders:* Tel: 416 597 1616
                800 815 9417
          Fax: 416 597 1617)

Australia
Blackwell Science Pty Ltd
54 University Street
Carlton, Victoria 3053
(*Orders:* Tel: 03 9347 0300
          Fax: 03 9347 5001)

A catalogue record for this title is available
from the British Library

ISBN 0-632-04151-X

Library of Congress
Cataloging-in-Publication Data
Brearley, Gill.
    Counselling children with special needs/
Gill Brearley.
        p. cm.
    Includes bibliographical references and
index.
    ISBN 0-632-04151-X
    1. Physically handicapped children—
Counseling of—Case studies. 2. Mentally
handicapped children—Counseling of—
Case studies.
HV903.B73   1997
362.4'083—dc21   97-8094
                                            CIP

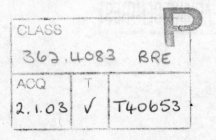

This book is dedicated to Peter Birchley and Robert Fisher.

Peter, much of whose life was involved in helping children. His imagination and insight made him a valued and exciting colleague.

Rob, whose work on his journey towards an early death taught me so much. I promised you would not be forgotten, Rob.

'So wise so young, they say, do never live long.'

Contents

Acknowledgement

This book would not have been written without the unfailingly patient and humorous encouragement, support, discussion, constructive criticism, faith and help with painstaking correction of drafts from Patrick Meighan.

Chapter 1
The Framework and the Subject

It may be helpful to the reader to understand some of the thinking behind the structure of this book and to appreciate the philosophy involved in its writing.

The form

The sequence of chapters aims to introduce information and examples of the skills a counsellor will need, in a way that will explain the techniques used by the counsellor in the case studies. When read in sequence, the information, discussion, examples and techniques should complement each other. Chapters can be selected and read in isolation, while cross-references within a chapter link it to other parts of the book.

Chapters relating to the direct effects of disability include Chapters 2, 3 and 4. Emotional implications are included in Chapters 5 to 11 while specific counselling skills are described in Chapters 12 to 15.

The model

Finding a model for the discussion of issues involving disability is always a problem. After considering a number of options, the model of bereavement seemed to be a useful one when considering the emotional needs of some children and young people with special needs and this is the model that has been selected.

This in no way assumes that every person with a disability or disabling illness experiences bereavement or has emotional problems connected with disability. The children described in this book, however, have experienced emotional difficulties directly related to disability and impairment, and it is to explore the counselling needs of these and others like them that is the purpose of this book.

The children

'Counselling children with special needs' implies a specific client group with needs that can be addressed by the counselling process. The suggestion is that children with special needs also have special problems, and special skills are required to enable resolution of these problems. These suggestions need more examination.

Children, or children and young people, can be defined as those who are learning the skills necessary for adult life. These skills include the practical, social, intellectual, emotional and moral. Practical skills include the development of physical strength, control and dexterity and the learning of procedures and methods. Social skills include learning the behaviours and communication acceptable to the society in which the child lives. Intellectual skills commence with learning cause and effect, and progress through the acquisition of specific abilities in accumulating facts, making connections, thinking and reasoning. Emotional development implies the achievement of balance and control of feelings. Moral skills may be defined as an awareness of and respect for the needs and rights of other people and may involve the specific demands of religion or culture.

Children with a variety of impairments may find it difficult to acquire any or all of these skills, perhaps even impossible. They may need extra help in learning what more able children achieve naturally, or special equipment to improve mobility and communication. Children with a physical or sensory impairment or a learning difficulty often need additional time and particular teaching methods to enable learning. Expectations may be lower, and some physical or intellectual skills may be impossible to achieve. Experiences can be restricted while demands made on them differ from their able peers. Children with recognised emotional or behavioural difficulties may have problems with learning and relationships.

In most developed societies it is accepted that children with special needs require extra resources and support in order to achieve their physical and intellectual potential. However, attitudes to such children are often very different from those experienced by their able peers. Even in the most enlightened societies a child who is obviously different can experience rejection, over-protection, mockery, pity, being patronised and underestimated, indulged or ignored. Some children will survive such experiences and achieve a wholeness and balance, but others will not. These will either struggle towards adulthood with pain and difficulty or will fail to develop some or all of the emotional and social skills needed for adult life. Learning and intellectual development can be difficult or impossible when a child experiences emotional problems.

Counselling

Counselling can help to resolve some of the emotional pain and difficulty where problems such as those discussed above are experienced. The availability of counselling can also help people working with children who have special needs, who may deny or not recognise problems. Denial may be a protection for the adult who feels unable to cope with the idea of children experiencing emotional pain and grief. Feeling unable to help or the fear of exposing unresolvable pain can lead to a refusal, albeit subconscious, to recognise problems. Stereotyping of particular disabilities can provide a comfortable explanation as, for example, the irritability and emotional instability associated with spastic hemiplegia. While those experienced with disability will recognise certain patterns of emotional problem associated with specific disabilities, to deny help on that basis is totally unacceptable.

Experience shows that there is a very great need for skilled counselling specifically for children with special needs. Some difficulties can be easily resolved, others considerably relieved. Intractable problems do exist. No counsellor can remove the limitations, pain and restrictions imposed by disability or illness. However, in the same way that counselling cannot bring back someone who has died but can help the survivor learn to live with his bereavement, counselling can help the disabled child to learn to live with his disability. With his emotional needs recognised and accepted, the child with disability, impairment or illness is enabled to develop the other areas of his learning.

The ability of the child to benefit from counselling depends on a number of factors. Age is not necessarily one of these. Children under three years old can be aware of difficult and painful feelings and can respond to counselling. 'Games' and directed play are valuable here. Children are often referred for counselling because of a perceived 'need' for such intervention. Older children and young people parti- cularly must have a choice and adults must be made aware that counselling is not effective unless it is a partnership between counsellor and client. Neither is counselling usually effective if presented as an alternative to punishment or exclusion. It is often accepted by a child as an adjunct to punishment – 'What you have done is wrong and you must be punished. I feel that you are not happy behaving as you are. Do you think it would help you to know why these things have happened? The counsellor may be able to help you.'

Some children may be unable to benefit from counselling because of severe intellectual impairment or very limited attention span. Some forms of brain damage, for example, seem to affect a child's sense of reality or their ability to make connections or retain information.

An example

Some children are unable or unwilling to trust the counsellor. It is important with any child that time be given to establish a good rela- tionship and not to expect or demand confidences too early in the relationship. One boy, Peter, severely disabled with cerebral palsy and non-verbal, had for several years been labelled as learning disabled and behaviourally disturbed. At twelve, when he was referred for coun- selling, only his parents and one or two school staff felt he was extremely intelligent and incorrectly handled. The first session with the counsellor seemed to confirm all the negative reports. Peter screamed and thrashed around, tipping his wheelchair dangerously. The coun- sellor unstrapped his restraints and allowed him to 'knee walk' around the room. He made a beeline for the sink, managed to hit the lever tap and sprayed water all over himself and the room, shrieking with laughter and screaming. He swept everything off a low shelf and attempted to drag a television off its stand.

The counsellor held him firmly and repeated a 'bargain' for the sessions. Peter could come out of his wheelchair if he did not wreck the room. He could play with the water if he did not squirt it. The coun- sellor would bring in games if he did not damage them. Eventually

Peter quietened enough to listen and finally said 'yes', he agreed to the bargain. The counsellor was pleased with the session and felt progress had been made. Indeed, at the next session Peter did behave as agreed after initially 'testing' the counsellor's resolve. However, the next six sessions showed no apparent progress. Peter refused to use his communication system, screamed and laughed when she attempted to suggest things he might find difficult and spent all the session playing with water or examining picture cards and books.

In supervision the counsellor reported that she felt the sessions were wasted. Peter did not want to confide in her and there was no movement at all in their relationship. The only positive thing was Peter's obvious eagerness to come to the sessions. The supervisor felt that this was very positive indeed, given the past reports, and advised that the sessions continue.

In the next session, Peter was thoughtful. He searched the box of games and asked for the picture cards to be spread on the floor. He slowly selected five cards and without looking at her, pushed them towards the counsellor. He had chosen cards depicting feelings – sad, happy, angry, scared and frustrated. The counsellor sat beside him and asked casually, 'Who are these people?' She drew symbols for various people on a piece of card and picked up the 'happy' picture. 'Is this happy person you, I wonder?', she mused. Peter shook his head, watching her intently. When she eventually asked, 'Is it me?' he agreed strongly. The counsellor laughed, 'Well. I am happy now because I like working with you. But (selecting and showing the appropriate cards) I sometimes feel sad, sometimes frustrated, often angry, sometimes scared. Like most people would, I suppose.' Peter quietly vocalised, 'yes'.

During the long and very productive counselling relationship which followed, Peter demonstrated a keen intelligence and awareness and an ability to make progress in his emotional development and general learning. He retained his freedom to decide whether or not to share his feelings, and in his occasional amiable refusal to discuss issues demonstrated a wicked sense of humour.

The other children

Peter is one of a number of children with special needs discussed in the following chapters, all of whom received counselling for a variety of problems. All names used are fictitious and some details (irrelevant to the counselling process) changed to protect identities. The children concerned have agreed for their counselling experiences to be used in this book. Their hope is that this will make counselling available to other children to help resolve their special needs and difficulties.

The style

Throughout the book, except in the case studies, the pronoun 'he' is used for the child and 'she' for the counsellor. This is entirely for clarity and convenience and in no way implies any stereotyping or assumptions. Similarly, the words 'child' and 'children' refer to all ages from birth to school leaver.

Where dialogue is reported, the counsellor's words are in standard print and the child's in italics.

Jargon and technical abbreviations have been avoided except when terms specific to the subject are necessary. These are defined within the script and included in the glossary. Jargon tends to be excluding and exclusive and as such has no place in a book designed to be accessible and informative.

Chapter 2
Some Typical Problems

Early development and influences

Many children with congenital disability have a history of problems from birth. Intensive care, early surgery, feeding difficulties, respiratory problems are all common experiences of babies with brain damage or spina bifida. Prematurity, with all its related risks, is a common factor of many children with cerebral palsy.

These early experiences have emotional as well as physical significance. The 'normal' baby will have experiences that establish certain emotional learning. A look at feeding will clarify this.

Hunger is a distressing experience. The baby will at first be restless, moving his head, rooting and seeking for the nipple, sucking at anything his mouth encounters. As hunger increases and the baby is unable to find satisfaction he will begin to scream, thrash around with all four limbs and generally express his overwhelming need for satisfaction. At some stage in this process, the mother (or other primary carer) will respond: the baby is picked up, reassured and fed. The baby experiences pleasure, satisfaction and an association with the smell, and later, appearance of the person who provides this satisfaction. As the baby develops, he will reach out for the breast or bottle and begin to consciously 'ask' for food. He will also experience and express anger if his needs are not quickly met.

The child born with brain damage may well be denied this early learning or may make negative associations that can damage subsequent learning. He may be tube fed and so not experience hunger and satisfaction. Inability to suck or to coordinate swallowing may make feeding a frustrating and distressing experience of hunger, choking and vomiting and denial of satisfaction. The mother, unable to meet her

7

baby's most basic need, will become distressed, despairing or angry. She will experience distress at her baby's distress, despair at her inability to comfort him and anger at the baby's apparent rejection of her. She may well be unable to cuddle and soothe her baby and an important bonding opportunity will then be denied.

A child who is severely learning disabled may have similar problems. A child unable to move around freely has difficulty in learning about his own relationship to the world around. This can affect the basic learning that precedes the acquisition of language, reading and mathematical skills as well as making it difficult for the child to achieve the necessary separation of himself from his surroundings and to become an individual with the ability to make choices and influence his surroundings. To a small baby, people who move out of his field of vision cease to exist: a child prevented by disability from exploring his environment may never develop a realistic understanding of the separateness of other people.

A child as young as two years can recognise differences between himself and other children. A child who is disabled can experience strong negative feelings about his difference. This awareness may not dawn until the child is older (in one case, a very severely disabled child did not experience any distress about her disability until twelve years old).

Effects of society

A teenager with cerebral palsy once said, 'I can't decide whether to become a PBC or a Supercrip.' When asked to explain, she said, 'Well, it's one or the other, isn't it? People either want you to be a Poor Bloody Cripple, holding your collecting box and having your head patted, or a Supercrip, climbing Mount Everest in a wheelchair or piloting Concorde with no arms.' Her friend was sceptical. 'It doesn't matter which you choose as long as you smile,' he declared. 'Happy happy, that's what they want.'

We do indeed, as a society, prefer a child with disability to be happy. We feel better and we protect ourselves from the pain of recognising the grief and frustration felt by such children at some time in their lives. We do not prefer. We demand.

A crying child in a wheelchair is more likely to be exhorted to cheer up than to be cuddled and sympathised with. All too often he will hear such remarks as, 'Such a happy child ... isn't it wonderful how happy they are, always smiling.' It pays to please powerful adults, especially when dependent on them and children learn quickly that a smiling face does please.

Why do we do this? As has been suggested, it is to protect ourselves. An able child distressed because of a fall or a pain can be comforted or distracted and 'made better'. A child distressed because he cannot walk or speak or because congenital deformity attracts unpleasant attention cannot be easily made better. We are helpless to alter the situation that hurts. It is easier to deny the hurt, to believe that children who are disabled have an associated predilection for happiness, an inability to understand their limitations.

A refusal to expose the child to reality is another aspect of this need to protect ourselves. Terrible distress has been caused to children told that one day they will walk/talk/be better again. Children have been told that an operation will work miracles (against all the evidence) or that a new treatment will restore functions. Of course we all want to believe and those close to the child sometimes need to convince themselves that the impossible is possible, but for professionals to collude is extremely damaging.

It is sometimes argued that to destroy hope is unforgivable. The issue is not, though, the destruction of hope. What is unacceptable is the deliberate creation of false hope.

Sandra, ten, had severe cerebral palsy and was non-verbal. Her teacher was very concerned because Sandra repeatedly told her that she would soon be able to walk, talk and use her hands. A talk with Sandra's parents did not help as they were unable to accept that she would not do all these things 'sometime' and anyway did not see any harm in Sandra believing this, 'She's only a baby.'

Sandra started refusing to use her communication system and to learn the skills needed to use a switch, which was an important stage in the possibility of Sandra being able to use an electric wheelchair, computer and environmental control system in the future. The help of the counsellor was requested.

Sandra was asked if she knew what cerebral palsy was, and she clearly did not. She was fascinated by pictures and explanation, and when she was asked if, knowing that damaged brain cells could not repair themselves, parts of the body controlled by those cells could recover, was pleased to know the answer was 'No.'

At the next session Sandra was proud that she could answer questions about her last session and wanted to know more. The counsellor began to suggest more positive aspects.

'Someone with cerebral palsy who couldn't speak can communicate with?'
'Blissymbols!'
'Someone who couldn't walk could get around in an?'
'Electric wheelchair.'
'Someone who couldn't use their hands could learn to use another part of their body to work a?'
'Switch!'

The counsellor then told Sandra about an adult friend with a similar disability to Sandra who used switches to drive his electric wheelchair and to operate a voice synthesiser. Would Sandra like to invite him to visit the school? Sandra asked the counsellor to help her write a letter and later proudly told her teacher, *'Man similar me have switch to talk to drive wheelchair come school to talk.'*

She did not refer again to herself talking or walking or using her hands. She no longer needed to deny her disability. She had the hope of acquiring the skills of her new friend. She did of course have painful and difficult feelings to work through but was saved the greater anguish of facing these later when false hopes had become more established.

Parents' feelings

The experiences of the parents of a child who is disabled are sometimes not fully understood or recognised. The parent of a boy of eight with spina bifida identified over thirty people who were involved in her family, from medical, paramedical, educational and social service agencies. She said bitterly, 'All these experts telling us what to do. Most people just have their mother and mother-in-law knowing best but I have all these as well. They all criticise but very few of them explain.'

Parents have described traumatic experiences connected with first learning that their child is damaged. These vary from their concerns being dismissed, sometimes for years, with accusations of being over-anxious or attention-seeking, to the information that their child will never be anything but a cabbage and they had better put it in a home and forget it and have another baby.

These examples may be extreme, but they do happen. Even when breaking the news is handled sensitively, parents are not usually able to absorb more than a few words before shock or denial cuts them off from what they are being told. A few members of the medical pro-fession do see parents a number of times and give opportunity for questions, but many parents have no idea what to ask. Some of the questions are almost impossible to ask aloud. Is it my fault? What did we do wrong? Why me? Who can I ask to deny it has happened?

Most mothers, even those who work with babies or have happily looked after those of friends or relatives, will tell of the panic they experience when they are at home alone with their own first baby. The responsibility seems overwhelming and the sense of inadequacy terri-fying. The most efficient people have confessed to telephoning their GP when their new baby sneezed and of scouring the baby books for information about what to do if their baby slept too much, or too little. It is difficult to imagine the feelings of the parents of a baby whom they have been told has cerebral palsy or spina bifida, previously only words associated with pathetically handicapped children in charity appeals. They are alone at home with the damaged child they have been given in place of the perfect baby they were expecting. Expected not just to manage but to understand and meet the special needs of this child, they often have to cope alone not only with their own feelings of inadequacy and ignorance but the fear, guilt, grief and anger of bereavement (see Chapter 6).

Parents with such feelings are not in the best position to meet their child's emotional needs. Add the sometimes overwhelming physical demands of a baby with disability and it is not surprising that some children with congenital disabilities suffer emotional deprivation, neglect and sometimes emotional abuse, however unintentional.

It must never be forgotten that a child who is disabled comes from a family that will be affected by that disability. The child may have complex needs, but so do the parents and siblings. The majority of families do their very best for a child that they love and care about. Blame for emotional problems experienced by the child is at best inappropriate, at worst very damaging. Understanding the situation, acknowledging the difficulties for the whole family, and offering support, if appropriate, may be the best way of helping the child.

When a child acquires a disability later in childhood, some of the same feelings and problems are experienced. Anger may be directed at another person; at a negligent doctor or a careless driver, at the mother or father themselves, for failure to notice illness, for carelessness, for neglect. The situation is still bereavement, in this case, of the child that was before the accident or illness. In addition the parent has to cope with the grief and anger of their child and of major changes in their life.

Having looked briefly at some developmental and emotional problems of a child disabled early in life and the feelings experienced by the parents of a child who is disabled, it is appropriate to review some possible emotional effects associated with specific disabilities.

Specific disabilities

Cerebral palsy

Cerebral palsy is the name given to a group of conditions caused by brain damage before, during or immediately after birth. As well as the effects of the main types of cerebral palsy described below, emotional effects due to epilepsy, perceptual problems and delayed development due to lack of physical exploration and limited experience may be apparent.

Spastic cerebral palsy

This results from damage to the cortex (the outer layer of the brain). Raised muscle tone results in stiffness affecting some or all muscles. Problems with spatial perception and body awareness are common. Speech may be slow and distorted. Reactions may be slow. Thinking processes may be slow and intelligence is often affected.

The damage described in detail in the section on spina bifida below resulting in the 'cocktail party syndrome' also affects some children with spastic cerebral palsy.

Emotionally, slowness and rigidity of thinking may make relationships difficult. He may perseverate, finding it difficult to leave a subject or continually return to it. One child described this as 'my needle gets stuck'. Change causes problems and stereotyped thinking is common.

The child affected by spasticity in these ways needs time and repeated explanation and support to accept change and assimilate new ideas. He may perceive the need for change as criticism and rejection, resulting in distress and obstinacy or even violence.

Ataxic cerebral palsy

This results from damage to the cerebellum (at the base of the brain). Coordination and balance are affected and there may be marked tremor and uncertainty of movement. Intelligence can be severely affected.

The child with ataxia may be timid and restricted emotionally. New experiences are very frightening and he may be slow in establishing relationships. Obsessive behaviour may be used to establish a 'safe' area.

Athetoid cerebral palsy

This is caused by damage to the basal ganglia (in the mid-brain). Movement is uncoordinated and 'overflow' of muscle stimulation causes unwanted movement which may be continuous. Speech may be severely affected. Hearing may be impaired. Intelligence is often not affected although learning can be impaired by physical limitations and perceptual problems.

The child with athetoid cerebral palsy may try very hard to control excess movements: this can lead to an increase in unwanted muscle activity and subsequent frustration. Unequal muscle tension and violent spasms can cause acute discomfort and pain with deformities (particularly of the hips and spine) developing.

Emotional control may be equally labile and a child with athetosis may overreact and find it hard to stop laughing or crying. Stress, excitement or anxiety may all trigger uncontrollable emotional reaction. When laughter results from teasing and jokes it can quickly become beyond control and cause distress.

Perseveration may be apparent. A less common but very difficult emotional 'overflow' results in paradoxical expression of emotion. The same exaggerated reactions occur but the opposite emotion to that experienced is expressed. Grief, fear, tension, anger may all result in wild laughter. The child is very aware of the inappropriateness of his reaction. That awareness and the disapproval of observers cause the child embarrassment and distress. His embarrassment and distress increase his reaction, his laughter becomes louder and more uncontrolled and the effects spiral. Such episodes can end with screaming and violent spasms which are often interpreted as a tantrum at being criticised.

Epilepsy

Epilepsy is commonly associated with disabilities caused by brain damage but may also be a condition in isolation. Children with epilepsy may experience frequent petit mal attacks, momentary losses of awareness, and/or grand mal attacks, losing consciousness and muscle control with spasmodic and violent muscle contractions.

Petit mal can cause confusion (the child being unaware he has experienced 'absences' or has 'missed') and irritation. Some children with grand mal may be fearful of precipitating an attack and display extreme timidity or may be reckless and resentful of control. Irritability, elation, depression or other unusual behaviour may be apparent before a grand mal attack.

Spina bifida

Spina bifida is a condition resulting from faulty development of the spinal column in the foetus. The bony arch of one or more vertebrae fails to form and damage to the spinal cord results. Frequently there is associated hydrocephalus, increased cerebrospinal fluid causing pressure on the brain. A valve is usually implanted to drain the fluid. Blocked valves can cause irritability, confusion, headache, blurred vision or nausea. Any unusual behaviour should always be investigated for valve blockage.

Complete or partial paralysis and a loss of sensation below the spinal damage will be present. Incontinence is a common result of spinal cord damage. Puberty is often very early in girls (menstruation may occur as early as eight years) but may be delayed in boys. Some boys do not develop secondary sexual characteristics and as men will be impotent and sterile. Both early and late puberty can cause distress and worry.

Some children with spina bifida may emotionally deny the existence of the paralysed parts of their body, neglecting personal hygiene and care and rejecting independence training in these areas. Such denial may also result in exaggerated unrealistic expectations and claims of achievement, to the extent that some children seem to inhabit a world that bears little or no relationship to what we perceive as reality.

Damage to the brain caused by hydrocephalus may result in the 'cocktail party syndrome'. The child may have a very sophisticated and elaborate vocabulary and pick up phrases and complex expressions with great facility but without any real understanding and will be unable to develop or maintain an idea. He is often unable to relate information learnt in one context to a different situation or to understand a sequence of events or remember a series of actions required to perform a given task. This can affect all areas of life; learning to read, achieving personal living skills, forming relationships, organisation and memory. Demands in these areas may evoke anger, excuses, depression or fierce defence.

Some brain damage in cerebral palsy can have the same effect.

Head injury

The brain damage following severe head injury can cause serious emotional as well as physical effects. Loss of short- and middle-term memory, emotional lability, irritability, anger, ritualistic behaviour, obsessive actions, loss of inhibition, inability to concentrate, can all result from traumatic brain damage.

However, many if not most survivors of severe head injury will also experience grief, anger, bewilderment, fear, frustration and despair at what has happened to them and will need sensitivity and understanding in this. Memory loss may mean that explanation and reassurance (but *not* false promises) will need frequent repetition.

Muscular dystrophy

Muscular dystrophy does not demonstrate its effects until the child is four or five years old, when muscle weakness begins to show. This may affect specific muscle groups and develop very slowly. One type is comparatively rapid in development and affects all muscle groups. This is Duchenne's muscular dystrophy, which affects only boys and is usually fatal in early manhood or sooner. Death is usually from a chest infection, the muscles being too weak for effective breathing or coughing, or from a heart attack, the heart being weakened by the condition.

Emotionally, the child is dealing with a terminal illness and is usually well informed. Many will attend a school or clinic where they will have seen the physical deterioration and death of the older boys with Duchenne's. A boy with Duchenne's will be very aware of his own increasing weakness and even if he does not ask direct questions will make an accurate assessment of the likely outcome of his illness.

Occasionally denial is the way chosen to cope with the situation.

Sometimes he may deal with his increasing weakness and help-lessness by verbal aggression and violent fantasies. Intelligence may be used aggressively and other people challenged and 'put down', as the child with Duchenne's uses the only strength he has to assert himself.

Cystic fibrosis

Cystic fibrosis is a congenital condition where mucus secretions are thickened and sticky, causing digestive problems and lung congestion. The child with cystic fibrosis will be on continual medication and a twice or three times daily regime of physiotherapy to keep the lungs clear. Many have frequent periods of hospitalisation.

As with Duchenne's muscular dystrophy, most children with cystic fibrosis will have knowledge that they have a terminal illness. In addition they often feel ill, are in extreme discomfort and are frustrated by the demands of their treatment. Some may be, or may become, depressed and negative.

Cancer

The protocol for treating cancer in children usually includes honesty and information. A child with leukaemia, for example, will usually respond better to painful and distressing treatment when he is informed about what is being done and why. Questions will be encouraged and answered honestly. In this climate a child is more likely to trust the medical staff and to cooperate in his treatment regime. Most children with cancer have periods of hospitalisation when they will observe and talk to other children and will often experience the death of a peer. Their feelings will be acknowledged and understood and support will be given. When the child returns home and to school, his way of dealing with the situation must be respected. If he wishes to talk about his illness this should be allowed at appropriate times. If he denies any difficulties this strategy should not be challenged. However, it must be made clear to the child that the possibility of causing distress to those he might confide in does not mean that his confidences are unwanted.

Learning difficulties

This rather blanket term has been used to describe very specific conditions, such as dyslexia, and global difficulties that were previously classified as 'mental handicap'. This summary is concerned with the latter.

Many children become aware at a very young age that they are 'different' from other children and most seem to have words like stupid, thick, and lazy in their vocabulary, often used as referents to themselves. Impatience, or exaggerated patience, of others when the child fails to grasp a simple instruction is something many of them are very aware of. It is not surprising that a low self-esteem is common, which may manifest as passivity, avoidance, sadness, irritability and aggression or defensive strategies.

Some common disabilities and their possible emotional effects have been briefly described.

A knowledge of normal child development and the effects of disability on that development will help the counsellor to understand some of the difficulties that may be experienced by a child who is disabled. An understanding of the possible emotional effects of specific disabilities and illnesses will enhance the counsellor's ability to empathise with a child who is disabled or ill. However, it must be remembered that whatever the cause, we all experience the same emotions. When someone is experiencing grief or anger what they feel is intense sadness or rage. The emotion is universal and the feeling is the same whether the person is a middle-aged policeman or a small girl in a wheelchair. The emotions of a child are as valid and significant to the child as the same emotions are to an adult.

The cause of difficult emotions is of course important and the recognition and acknowledgement of the cause is the first step towards resolution. This is the counselling process. It is the same regardless of whether the client is able or disabled, adult or child, male or female. Different enabling skills may be needed in different circumstances.

Chapter 3
The Child with Communication Problems

Communication and disability

All human contact demands communication in some form or another. When two people meet, speech is perhaps the most obvious way in which they communicate but there are many other more subtle ways in which they give information. For instance, the tone, speed, volume and inflection of their words, the way they dress, their gesture and expression, their stance and body position and the nature of their eye contact all communicate information to another.

Where there is disability some of these communication signals may be distorted and misread. For example, a body stance where the arms are held close to the body, the head is bowed and the knees held close together state in body language, 'Keep off, don't try and get close to me.' A person with spastic cerebral palsy will usually have a body distorted into such a shape by spasm of the flexor muscles. They will be inadvertently communicating 'keep off' and anyone approaching them will be subconsciously influenced by this message. Another example helps explain why someone with severe cerebral palsy can be infantilised. A baby communicates helplessness, vulnerability, the need for care. A baby cannot speak but his wide eyes, gaping mouth, dribbling, uncoordinated movements and waving limbs are powerful communicators that adults instinctively respond to. Someone with athetoid cerebral palsy may present a very similar picture to that of the helpless baby and may experience the same response.

Communication between adults and children may experience difficulties. There may be a difference in vocabulary and therefore a problem of comprehension. The attitude of the adult, the tone and inflection of speech, can easily antagonise a child who feels patronised and demeaned. No child wishes to be spoken to in the tones of the late Joyce Grenfell as the teacher in her nursery school sketch but it is possible to observe versions of that lady in many day-to-day examples of adults talking to children. Many people who regard someone with a disability as disenfranchised adopt such tones in speaking to a person in a wheelchair or a person similarly clearly disabled in some way. When the disabled person is also a child the block to communication can be greatly increased.

Counselling depends on communication between the counsellor and the client. The counsellor needs to communicate acceptance, warmth and empathy. The client needs to communicate his feelings and concerns. The counsellor working with children needs to develop special communication skills and when that child is disabled she must be aware of some important considerations affecting communication.

Race and culture

Children in an English-speaking community whose first language is not English, especially when the first language is that spoken at home, may have communication difficulties with an English-speaking counsellor. In addition, a home life of a different culture and tradition can lead to difficulties if the counsellor does not understand the significance of these.

Dr John Collee, in an article in *The Observer* (7 January 1996), makes this point in relation to intelligence tests. In devout Jewish and Muslim families, he records, children would not be allowed to see a picture of a pig, an unclean animal. They would not recognise a pig in a test picture. A colleague of Dr Collee, Dr Bashir Qureshi, points out that to a fundamentalist Muslim, anything made to resemble a life form is forbidden. A teddy bear or doll may be extremely offensive.

These are perhaps extreme examples. However, a counsellor can learn awareness from such information. A teenage boy with cerebral palsy worked well in counselling, cooperating and showing considerable insight into his feelings of anger and frustration. Nevertheless, his attitude to the counsellor outside the sessions was very aggressive, the boy seeming to seek her out to make offensive remarks and sneering comments. When she talked about this to a colleague from the same country of origin as the boy, she learned that, in his culture, women were regarded as subservient to men and to be helped by a woman was deeply shaming. The boy needed and valued his counselling but also needed to restore what he perceived as a loss of face by showing his scorn for her. She suggested a transfer to a male colleague and he accepted. His attitude to her changed completely and he greeted her with every appearance of courteous friendship. If she had understood his situation from the beginning a great deal of distress could have been avoided.

The attitude towards disability by different cultures can vary widely and must be understood.

Language disorders

Damage to the brain areas concerned with language can lead to communication difficulties. The damage may be congenital, sustained during birth or be the result of disease or trauma. It may be associated with other disabilities caused by brain damage or may be specific to language.

A child with a language disorder may have difficulty understanding what he hears or may be unable to express what he wants to say. This difficulty can take a wide variety of forms, both general and specific. When working with a child with language disorder it is essential to consult the speech and language therapist involved with the child to obtain an explanation of the problem and the best ways of communicating with that particular child.

Developmental delay in the acquisition and understanding of language may affect some children. Although children with learning difficulties usually have a delay in language development, it must be emphasised that language delay is not necessarily a reflection of the intelligence of the child. The counsellor will need to use simple language, avoid complex sentences and not ask multiple questions or give several commands in one sentence. This does not mean using 'baby-talk' or special inflection or intonation. For example, to say 'I wonder if you could take off your outdoor clothes and then you might like to sit down over there on the blue plastic chair', would be very difficult for the child to understand. To simplify the instructions and to give them one at a time, waiting until the child has complied with each step before going on, will help. 'Take off your hat. Good. Take off your coat. Right. Do you see the chairs? Yes. Can you point to the blue one? Good. Go to the blue chair. That's right. Sit down.' Reinforcing your instructions with a gesture or an action (point to the chair or go there yourself) helps the child to understand and praise or confirmation when he gets it right will encourage him and give him confidence.

Speech difficulties

A disabled child may have intact language but difficulties with speech, or he may have speech difficulties and a language disorder. Lack of muscle coordination or muscle spasm, as in cerebral palsy, will affect breath control and the muscles of articulation. The speech of a cerebral palsied child may be very slow and fragmented making it difficult to understand. It may be produced in a series of rapid and hurried phrases. Words may be mispronounced or distorted, with some consonants missing. The child may attempt to speak when breathing in or when he has no breath to articulate. The child may be unable to articulate at all or may be unable to produce any sound. Delay or disorder in the ability to produce words or word sounds may also occur, with or without language delay.

Deformities of the mouth and palate will affect the clarity of speech. Stammering sometimes occurs. A child whose speech is often not understood may be reluctant to talk. Sometimes reluctance to speak may also be due to the child's facility in communicating with pointing and gesture which he finds quicker and easier than speech. Children whose parents anticipate their every need and talk for them may not be motivated to speak.

It can take a little time to 'tune in' to difficult speech. It is essential for the counsellor to be relaxed and to feel that there is no hurry. The counsellor should not feel deskilled or a failure if she does not understand at once. Very experienced professionals accustomed to difficult speech often have problems in understanding a child with speech problems. Never pretend to understand or hope that there will be a clue later that will make the message clear. If you do not understand, say so at once and ask the child to repeat what he has said. Take responsibility for not understanding and explain that you want to talk but will need time to get used to the child. Ask key questions when necessary to establish the subject. Speech-impaired children are used to people not understanding their speech and will not be distressed if they feel the counsellor wants to understand, has time and is relaxed.

Background noise, someone else interpreting and telling the child to take a deep breath or take his time are all unhelpful to the process of understanding.

It is not the counsellor's role to insist on speech when a child is reluctant to talk. Other ways of communicating are just as effective (see Chapter 12).

Alternative and augmentative communication (AAC)

Children with severe communication problems may use a variety of ways of communicating. This communication may be at any level from the most basic expression of practical needs to extremely sophisticated communication of thoughts and feelings. It is important for the counsellor working with a child using alternative or augmentative communication (AAC) to establish with the person most experienced in communicating with the child, the level of skill of the child and the method used. It may be helpful to observe, with the child's permission, a conversation between the therapist and the child.

When working with a verbal child, respect and confidentiality are essential. These criteria are the same for the non-verbal child. It can take a conscious effort to remember that a child who does not respond with speech nonetheless understands speech spoken normally appropriate to his age. It is deeply humiliating to an intelligent, non-verbal child to be spoken to in the loud, slow, exaggeratedly accented speech usually reserved by a certain type of person for toddlers, foreigners and those slow in understanding.

It is often a sad fact that the greater the disability of the child, the less respect is paid to his privacy. The Head of Care of a College of Further Education for students with physical disability and communication problems tells of having to reprimand staff for ignoring a student's right to privacy. Typical incidents included calling down a crowded corridor, 'Will you come and help with Joe – he needs a suppository' and 'Did you know Joe is wet again?' People often speak over the head of a non-verbal child as if he is not there and discuss him or other children as if he was unable to understand. This lack of respect can be evinced by professionals and parents, sometimes to an astonishing degree. In one example, the parents of an intelligent non-verbal child were horrified when the counsellor told them that their twelve-year-old son had communicated to her that he slept in his parents' bedroom and often observed them having intercourse. They had never thought that he was old enough to understand! In another case, a surgeon discussed with his team across the bed of an eleven-year-old, non-verbal child the poor prognosis of his condition. The surgeon expressed disbelief when he was informed that the deeply distressed child had relayed the conclusions to the counsellor.

Signing

British Sign Language (BSL), used by people with hearing impairment, is a complete language and only counsellors who have learnt and practised BSL are able to use it when counselling without an interpreter.

Makaton signs are derived from BSL and may be used by hearing children with speech problems to communicate simple needs and feelings. Adequate hand and arm control is necessary in order to make clear signs. Children with language problems may be helped to understand speech if signs are used in combination with simple words. Some children may use a combination of words, signs and gesture to communicate.

Symbols

Symbols or pictures can be used for communicating at a very basic level or can provide a sophisticated language for the user.

Communication at a very basic level may use photographs, drawings or Rebus symbols. Rebus symbols are stylised pictures representing objects and basic feelings. A child can use a Rebus chart or book to indicate concrete ideas and feelings but cannot communicate abstract ideas. For example, the Rebus symbol for 'talk' has the outline of a mouth with two wavy lines beside it.

The Mayer-Johnson Picture Communication System uses more sophisticated but still clearly recognisable pictures to communicate a wide range of word categories: people, verbs, nouns, descriptive, social and miscellaneous. Feelings and sexuality are included in a total of over 3000 pictorial symbols. The associated word is included above the drawing for the benefit of the person with whom the user is communicating.

Blissymbolics is a system of communication that uses pictograms and concept-based symbols that can be used at a basic, telegrammatic level or as a complete language capable of great subtlety and individuality. A Bliss user does need to interpret sounds or words to use Bliss effectively although some users will use grammatical sentences at a sophisticated level.

The word that a symbol represents is printed above the symbol in the user's chart or book for the benefit of the person to whom the user is talking. However, when the user is communicating at a high level he may want a very exact interpretation and the counsellor will need to check his exact meaning. For example, the symbol for 'to speak' can also be used for 'to say, to tell, to talk, etc.' The context will often give a clue to which word the user wants.

Accessing symbols

If the child has hand control, he will be able to point to the symbols. The counsellor can then simply repeat each symbol as it is indicated until she has the complete message.

A child unable to point, either with finger, knuckle, foot or other body part, will need to use eye-pointing. Initially, the counsellor must establish the way in which the child indicates 'yes' and 'no', by asking him to show each in turn. It is wise to make a note of this as the easiest movement each child can make will usually be used to indicate 'yes'. Some children may be able to verbalise a 'yeh' or 'uh' or give a clear nod of the head. For others a slow, controlled eye blink or looking upwards will indicate 'yes' or perhaps putting out the tongue. The sign for 'no' will be clearly different. The child may be able to say 'neh' or shake his head. A child who looks up for 'yes' may close his eyes for 'no'. Each child will use different responses according to which movements he finds easiest. If a child is only able to control one clear movement this will be used for a 'yes' response. The only reliable movement Julia could achieve was a slow eye-blink. Her 'no' was a lack of active response.

Having established the 'yes' and 'no' responses the counsellor will then use questions to enable the child to access the symbol system. Ideally the method the child uses will be described in his book or on his chart. The most common method is to first ask on which page of the book or area of the chart the symbol is situated, asking, 'Is it this page?' or 'Is it in this part of the chart?' until a 'yes' is given. Some children with symbol books are able to use an index in which case the page is identified from the index at the front of the book. Then the column in which the symbol is situated is identified in the same way, then the particular symbol. The process is repeated until the whole message is communicated. The child is asked if he has any more symbols when the message appears to be complete or when he indicates that it has ended.

Some children use a system of number or colour coordinates to access the location of symbols in their chart or book. It is important to check which method a child uses before starting to communicate, perhaps by observing the child talking to a teacher or speech and language therapist.

The message may be given as single words. A child unhappy because his grandfather has died may give the message 'sad grandfather'. The counsellor will need to reflect back what she thinks is meant, 'You are sad because of your grandfather?' If the child indicates 'yes' he may then be able to explain if requested, 'dead', or may need further questions in order for him to explain why he is sad about grandfather.

Alternatively the message may be in telegram form, 'I sad grandfather dead.'

The message may be in 'Bliss grammar'. It seems that many children who use Bliss do not think in grammatical sentences. Evidently the tendency is to indicate the symbols in the order of their importance to the child. The message may be given 'grandfather sad dead I', for example. This Bliss grammar has been observed in children whose native language has a very different grammatical structure, for example Polish children using Bliss.

It may be necessary again to question the child to ensure that the message has been received correctly. It helps to write down each symbol as it is given because it is easy to forget when the communication takes some time and may not immediately make sense.

It is very important that the counsellor does not assume that she knows what the child is saying and interrupt with her interpretation before the child has finished the message. It will confuse the child if the counsellor suggests the symbol she thinks will come next. Nor is it helpful to query a symbol that has been confirmed but does not seem relevant. If the whole message has been given and does not appear to make sense, check each symbol with the child. It may then be necessary to ask questions. 'You are telling me about grandfather? Is it grandfather that is sad? Is it you that is sad? Are you sad because of something to do with grandfather? Is someone dead? Is it grandfather that is dead? So you are feeling sad because grandfather has died.'

Although this may seem a tedious and slow method of communication when compared with the alternative, the posing of 'yes' or 'no' questions in an attempt to establish the broad area of concern and then attempting to narrow this down to the particular, it is infinitely more useful. This enables the child to say what he wants to communicate rather than accept an approximation or give up altogether.

Sometimes if the child is very upset or cannot make himself understood it may be necessary to ask questions. It is almost always very difficult to influence a child to accept an incorrect interpretation but there are safeguards against this. It is important to tell the child that you are going to guess and that you may make some very silly guesses. He will have to tell you every time if you are wrong. This may be difficult for the child so practice is not wasted time. For example, you know that the child's name is Warren. Ask, 'Is your name Caroline? Is your name Mickey Mouse? Is your name John?' before asking 'Is your name Warren?' Accept the responsibility for incorrect guesses and praise the child for clearly rejecting these.

The 'arrow method' of questioning, gradually narrowing the field, might then progress as follows. The child's responses are given in italics.

'Can you tell me how you are feeling? Is it happy?'
'No.'
'Is it angry?'
'No.'
'Is it sad?'
'Yes.'
'So you are feeling sad. Are you feeling sad about something that has happened?'
'Yes.'
'Is it something that has happened a long time ago?'
'No.'
'Is it something that happened a little while ago?'
'Yes.'

'More than a week ago?'

'No.'

'At the beginning of the week?'

'No.'

'Yesterday?'

'No.'

'The day before? Thursday?'

'Yes.'

'So you are feeling sad about something that happened on Thursday. Is it to do with school?'

'No.'

'Is it to do with home?'

'Yes.'

'Is it to do with family?'

'Yes.'

'Has something happened to mummy or daddy?'

'No.'

'Has something happened to brothers or sisters?'

'No.'

'Has something happened to you?'

'No.'

'Has something happened to granny or grandad?'

'Yes.'

'To one of them?'

'Yes.'

'To grandad?'

'Yes.'

'Is he ill?'

(uncertain response)

'Right, I will ask that differently. Has he been ill?'

'Yes.'

'Very ill?'

'Yes.'

'Has he been taken to hospital?'

'Yes.'

'Are we there? Is there more? Can you tell me if you have finished what you want to tell me?'

'No.'

'I am going to make a guess. I am very sorry if it is a wrong guess.

Sometimes when people are old and get very ill, they die. Did grandad die?'
'Yes.'

It is important to notice that questions can only be answered with a 'yes' or a 'no'. It is surprising how many people will ask an either/or question of a child who is able only to indicate 'yes' or 'no' and then be surprised that they do not get a clear answer.

Voice output communication aids

Children may use one of the large number of electronic communication aids available. They will access their voice output communication aid (VOCA) by hitting keys on a keyboard or with an optical or infrared head pointer or a switch operated by another part of their body. Depending on the skill and experience of the user, the aid supplied and their ability to access it, communication may be at a very basic level or at any stage up to the sophisticated type of VOCA that the reader may have heard being used by Professor Stephen Hawking. Spelling is not essential. VOCAs which use the Minspeak system (where special symbols are used), for example, do not depend on an ability to read or spell. Until a fair level of skill has been achieved most children prefer to use their symbol system in counselling. Some children will use their VOCA to greet the counsellor and will then ask for their symbol book. The choice must be theirs but if there is obviously a problem with the high-tech aid it would not be inappropriate to ask if he would prefer to use symbols.

The choice of AAC

Before any child begins to use AAC he will have been carefully assessed by experts in the field before a system is chosen. This assessment may be at a Communication Aid Assessment Centre such as the Wolfson Centre or ACE (Aids to Communication in Education), or by a school speech and language therapist. The speech and language therapist will test the child's level of language acquisition, his ability to make choices and his readiness to communicate. The therapist will consult the parents, the child, the teacher and the physiotherapist. Similarly the method used to indicate 'yes' and 'no' and the way a child accesses his system will have been carefully and lengthily assessed before a decision is made. It may be that the counsellor feels that there is an easier method but to suggest to a child, for example, that it would be better to smile and look at her for 'yes' can cause confusion and distress.

> Katie looked up for 'yes' and away for 'no'. The person talking to her had to concentrate as Katie saw no reason to repeat herself if her companion was not attending and missed the response. A new staff member instructed Katie to smile for 'yes' – smiling was easy for Katie and clear to the teacher. This led initially to confusion as Katie was using a smile in the classroom but her established sign in therapy and communication group. After a time Katie used only the smile as it was easier and also it was insisted on in the classroom. However, when problems arose in class it became very clear why the therapist and others involved had established the eye movement. When Katie was distressed and urgently needed to communicate she was unable to use her Bliss. She could not smile when she was crying and upset and could not indicate which symbols she wanted.

> Frank's classroom assistant encouraged him to smile for 'yes' instead of using a slow blink. When a member of the class was telling the teacher how miserable she felt because children in the park called her names, Frank eagerly signalled his sympathy and agreement with a strong 'yes', by smiling as he had been instructed. His friend burst into tears and said 'Frank's laughing at me.'

Not only is it a cause of confusion and distress, it is also arrogant for the counsellor or anyone else to propose alterations in the way someone communicates. It would be inconceivable to think of correcting a client's pronunciation or grammar in a counselling session. The AAC user should be accorded no less respect.

Communication with a child using any form of AAC needs practice and time. The counsellor needs to focus on the child and the system that the child is using and to be sensitive to the need for a relaxed attitude to time and success. The counsellor will need to accept that she may feel stupid and slow when she fails to understand and will need to realise that the most experienced communicator with AAC users will sometimes fail to understand a message. If the counsellor feels stressed, impatient or anxious this will be communicated to the child and will impede or even prevent communication. It is important to remember that, for the child, being with one person who is concentrating on him for a set period of time and wants to hear and understand what he has to say is in itself a valuable and affirming experience. To be treated witih respect and to have the dignity of having his ideas and feelings accepted and valued is healing and empowering. Once the counsellor accepts this and relaxes and feels confident, the 'real' counselling will develop.

Chapter 4
Sexuality and Relationships

Disability and sexuality

Sex education is usually regarded as ideally being the privilege of parents but practically the responsibility of schools.

The National Curriculum for schools in England and Wales includes sex education and 'family life education' in the Health Education Curriculum for children aged between five and sixteen years. Sex education is however required by the 1986 Education Act to be at the discretion of the school governors. Their duty is:

'...to consider separately...the question whether sex education should form part of the secular curriculum for the school...'

The Sex Education Forum, an independent body representing organisations involved in providing support and information to those who provide sex education to young people, includes in its statement of aims and beliefs the following:

'Sex education should:

- be an integral part of the learning process beginning in child-hood and continuing into adult life;
- be for all children, young people and adults, including those with physical, learning or emotional difficulties;
- encourage exploration of values and moral issues, consideration of sexuality and personal relationships and the development of communication and decision-making skills;
- foster self-esteem, self-awareness, a sense of moral responsibility and the skills to avoid and resist unwanted sexual experience.'

The policy statement of the Association to Aid the Sexual and Personal Relationships of People with a Disability (SPOD) begins:

'Every disabled person has the right to informed sex education and the dignity of an acknowledged sexual identity.'

'Every disabled person should have the opportunity to form relationships of their own choice.'

For many children, even these basic rights are not met. Many children attending schools for children with special needs do not receive even the most basic sex education. There are several reasons for this.

Many people still feel that disabled people do not have sexual feelings. This may be a denial, protecting the able person from contemplating the sexual difficulties they might perceive as facing a disabled person. It may be symptomatic of a need to keep disabled people as children, innocent and dependent – and therefore undemanding.

Others may accept that sexual feelings are possible but that their fulfilment is not. If there is a premise that a child will never be able to experience a sexual relationship (or is not going to marry, as many people assume rigid, moral expectations of disabled people) it would be unfair to give him information about what 'normal' people do.

Ignorance about how disability may affect sexual expression is also given as a reason for not teaching a basic sex education, 'I don't know if it will be possible for him', leading to the specious observation, 'What they don't know won't hurt them.' The myth that children will be ignorant of sexuality unless they are taught about it may seem extraordinary but has often been expressed. This not only ignores the content of many television programmes popular with children and shown before the so-called watershed but denies the awareness of sensations and needs felt by almost every growing child.

Some teachers take the view that they will answer questions when they arise. This statement is sometimes followed by the rather naive justification that such questions never do arise. Perhaps the opportunity and 'permission' to enable a child to ask about sex is never provided. How does the child know what to ask if he has been given no vocabulary with which to form his question?

Parental involvement

Parents may experience any of the reasons given above for not informing such a child about 'the facts of life'. They may also feel the diffidence and embarrassment of many parents in talking about sex with their own child. Parents may feel that their disabled child is too young to understand even when younger siblings are fully informed.

When their child has learning disabilities, parents may feel that sexual awareness is a dangerous thing and will lead to experimentation and the risk of trouble. This ignores the fact that in every other aspect of their lives knowledge is seen as positive and a protection from harm. A vulnerable or over-trusting child is far more able to behave safely if he is informed about sexuality and given simple guidelines for safety based on that knowledge.

In most family circles there will be someone – mother, aunt, cousin, neighbour – who is pregnant. The child who is disabled is often disregarded when pregnancy and childbirth are being discussed. He may overhear partial or inaccurate facts and frightening stories. He will piece together what he has heard and what he has observed and may build up an inaccurate and bewildering story.

The questions

Even when basic sex education is on the school curriculum, issues of disability are seldom raised. In a discussion group, teenagers with a variety of disabilities who had received sex education asked the following questions:

'Could I have sex?'
'Would I be able to have a baby?'
'Can you have sex when you have a catheter?'
'Would my baby have a handicap?'
'Can you have sex if you're incontinent?'
'If my girlfriend was disabled like me would anyone help us to have sex?'
'Do disabled people always marry other disabled people?'
'Could a disabled person get AIDS?'
'How can you put a condom on if you can't use your hands?'

'Are any disabled people gay?'
'Can a boy have sex if he doesn't get erections?'
'Does sex hurt if you're disabled?'
'What does sex feel like if you're paralysed?'

The counsellor

Unless there is an atmosphere in the school that encourages open discussion and an informed and accessible person to answer such questions, the counsellor may well be seen as a resource. It will be acceptable initially to say, 'I don't know,' but this must be followed with 'but I will find out.'

Resources for information are listed in the list of Useful Organisations at the back of this book. The school nurse will usually be willing to help with answers. The general practitioner may be able to give guidance. However, it may be necessary to contact either the specific organisation or SPOD, which has a series of resource and information leaflets. There is also a telephone helpline for professionals or the child himself may wish to contact one of the counsellors direct, either on the helpline or by letter.

Adolescence

With some exceptions which will be referred to, children with special needs go through the same process of puberty as their able peers. They will experience the same body changes and suffer the same mood swings. The counsellor will need to reassure the adolescent that these experiences are normal.

Dal was thirteen and his voice was beginning to break. Even allowing for adolescent 'moods', Dal appeared unduly depressed and irritable and was asked if he would like to speak to the counsellor. He rather grudgingly agreed and after some time asked abruptly, 'Does cerebral palsy get worse as you get older?' The counsellor reflected, 'You are worried that your disability might be getting worse?' Dal mumbled, 'Well – like – I've never wet the bed before.'

After talking to the counsellor it became apparent that what Dal was experiencing was nocturnal emission. When the counsellor explained about 'wet dreams' and congratulated Dal on his maturing body he became quite proud. He did ask that the counsellor explain to his parents and with the assurance that she would, ended the session happily.

Sarah thought that her bouts of crying and emotional outbursts meant that she was going mad. She had no knowledge of the hormonal effects of puberty. Encouraged to keep a diary of her moods, the link to menstruation was clear and she was much better able to cope.

Some disabilities affect the onset of puberty. Girls with spina bifida may enter menarche as early as seven or eight years old. This can cause great distress, the child being totally unprepared for menstruation and acutely embarrassed by the development of breasts and the appearance of acne. As with Dal, the counsellor may be able to help the child feel proud that her body is growing up and preparing for adulthood.

With boys who have spina bifida puberty may be delayed, sometimes until the early twenties, or in severe conditions, may not be achieved. Boys may become acutely aware that their penis has not developed and that they are not experiencing erections. The counsellor will need to judge whether information about sexual expression and satisfaction with an incomplete or absent erection will be appropriate. It may be more appropriate to give the information that the desired development is often delayed in spina bifida.

In cerebral palsy puberty may be delayed.

It is important to remember that severely disabled children may not have the opportunity to see their own bodies. The common teenage occupation of detailed self examination in a full length mirror will be denied them.

Linda confided to the counsellor that she would never become a woman. She was sixteen, she said, and her body was a little girl's body. The counsellor was initially puzzled: Linda clearly had hips and breasts. Then Linda was asked when she had last had a good look at herself in a long mirror. 'I never have,' was the reply. Linda was totally disabled with cerebral palsy. Baths and dressing were carried out by carers.

When Linda went swimming, with her eager agreement she was supported naked in front of a full length mirror. She stared at herself with dawning excitement and laughed up at her carer. 'Nice body. Better than mine, you lucky thing,' were the carer's comments.

Relationships

Children who attend a special needs school may have a very limited peer group. In a typical secondary school, there were twenty pupils over the age of fifteen. Twelve of these were boys. The intellectual range was from severe learning disability to above average. The physical disabilities ranged from very severe disability with no speech to slight uncoordination. Four pupils had moderate behaviour problems. Another had some autistic behaviours. Because most of the pupils were resident their social life was mostly centred in the school. As the pupils came from a wide catchment area they rarely saw fellow pupils during the holidays. In such circumstances, which are common, teenagers lack the experience of forming and breaking relationships, falling in and out of love, that usually will be the experience of their peers in mainstream education.

Even when a disabled child attends a mainstream school he may not be perceived by his peers as a possible boyfriend. Tammy had many friends but at fourteen wanted the more special girl–boy relationships that her friends were involved with. 'I know lots of boys,' she commented bitterly. 'They tell me all about their troubles with their girl friends.'

This lack of experience may be compounded by unreality in the relationships a child does experience. 'She's my sweetheart,' 'He's my boyfriend,' is sometimes said of children by adults caring for them. This is possibly an appropriate demonstration of affection when the child is two or three years old but when said of a ten-year-old or a young adult such phraseology can give rise to painful misapprehensions. It is disturbing when a fifteen-year-old girl confides that she and the fifty-year-old school gardener are in love and are going to get married when the listener knows that the man is totally unaware of such a fantasy.

Such failure to understand the nature of relationships can give rise to painful and embarrassing situations at best or a serious risk of exploitation at worst. Much unnecessary grief is caused by inappropriate approaches and assumptions and the young disabled adult may conclude that he is not able to form any real relationships. He may withdraw, become bitter, fantasise or make persistent and unwelcome advances. He may make impossible demands and be resentful when they are not met. He will need a great deal of help and guidance in developing awareness of the rights and responsibilities of personal relationships.

Sexual abuse

The idea that any adult could sexually abuse a child is abhorrent to most people but it is now widely accepted that it can and does occur. The sexual abuse of a disabled child is even more difficult to believe but almost certainly occurs more often than that of the able child. There are many possible reasons for this.

A child who has most or all of his physical needs met by an adult has difficulties in defining the boundaries of what is acceptable touching. For example, an incontinent child may be catheterised or wear incontinence pads. The use of a catheter or the cleaning of the genital area when a pad is changed involves intimate touching. How can a child distinguish between such necessary touching and that of abuse?

A disabled child is used to his body being manipulated and observed. Far too often no effort is made to respect the child's privacy and a child wishing to retain undergarments may be told 'Don't be silly'.

There is far more opportunity for an abusing adult to have access to a disabled child. When it is remembered that the majority of abusers are members of the abused child's family and that a disabled child often requires care and supervision long after an able child would be independent, the reason is obvious. It may be difficult to define the boundaries. For example, the reader may like to consider at what age it is no longer appropriate or desirable for a father to bath his disabled daughter. Will the decision be affected if the mother is physically unable to manage this task? There are no easy answers but it is clear that boundaries must be defined and drawn for the protection of the vulnerable child.

Non-verbal children or children with speech or language difficulties are especially vulnerable as they are often unable to tell what is happening even if they have the opportunity. They may well not have the vocabulary or understanding to convey what is happening.

Sylvia was nine, severely disabled with cerebral palsy and non-verbal. She was a Bliss user. She agreed to see the counsellor when her bouts of screaming and weeping seemed to have no discernible cause.

'Can you tell me how you are feeling?'
'Afraid. Angry.'
'You are afraid and angry. Can you tell me what that is about?'
'Bed.'
'Something to do with bed? Can you tell me any more?'
'Daddy.'
'Something to do with bed and with daddy? Can you tell me about that?'
'No.'
'Do you have the symbols?'
'Don't know.'
'Do you want me to ask questions?'
'Yes.'
'Is it your bed?'
'Yes.'
'Are you in your bed when you feel afraid and angry?'
'Yes.'
'Is daddy there?'
(no clear response)
'Can I make some guesses? I may make some pretty silly ones.'
'Yes.'
'Are you afraid of having the light out? Afraid of the dark?'
'No.'
'Do you think you are being put to bed when you want to stay up?'
'No.'
'You mentioned daddy. Is it to do with daddy when you are in bed?'
'Yes.'
'Where is daddy? In your bedroom?'
'Yes. Bed.'
'What – sitting on your bed?'
'No.'

'Lying on your bed?'

'Yes.'

'Is daddy angry with you when he is lying on your bed?'

(unclear response)

'Sylvia, can you give me any clues at all? I'm feeling a bit stuck. You said you were afraid and angry, that daddy is lying on your bed and you are in bed – but daddy is not angry with you.'

'Pencil.'

'Pencil? Is that the right symbol? Something to do with a pencil?'

'Pencil. Daddy.'

At this point the counsellor became very concerned. Sylvia had no symbols for sexual organs but the symbol for pencil (an upward slanting line) and the similarity of the word to 'penis' was suggesting that there was at least a possibility that Sylvia was describing abuse by her father.

'Sylvia, I am feeling a bit worried. It sounds as if you have something very important to tell but it is hard for you to communicate this.'

'Yes.'

'I think we may need someone else to help. Would it be OK if I asked [the person responsible for suspected abuse] to come and talk with us?'

'Yes.'

A careful interview followed with the questions and answers recorded. Because of having to avoid 'leading' Sylvia the results were still unclear but a strong suspicion was felt. A decision was taken to talk to the parents. Sylvia accepted this. In the event only the father attended the meeting. He was told that there was concern because Sylvia had communicated that she felt afraid and angry and that this was something to do with her father and bedtime. She was clearly very upset and the matter needed to be resolved. After protestations that nothing was wrong, the father eventually said that there had been 'some problems' but assured the counsellor and teacher that the difficulties were now over and wouldn't occur again. Sylvia had been difficult to settle at night, he said, and he had become impatient with her. He had refused to sit with Sylvia when she was in bed and Sylvia had become upset about this.

With the situation still equivocal, her father was told that Sylvia would continue to talk with the counsellor. He assured the meeting that he would be glad of this 'for Sylvia to get help'.

The responsible person was unable to come to any definite conclusion and advised 'keeping an eye on things' and contacting her if any further comment was made by Sylvia. At the next counselling session Sylvia said that she was happy and not angry or afraid any more. Her screaming bouts ceased.

The truth of the situation given above can only be speculated upon. It may well be that many acts of sexual abuse are perpetrated against non-verbal and severely disabled children but the legal safeguards against influencing a child's statements act against the needs of the non-verbal child.

The counsellor should always familiarise herself with the procedure established in any school or institution for suspected sexual abuse. If the child is not in a school or institution then any suspicions should be reported to the Social Services department in the area of the child's home. The possibility of this action will have been made clear in the original counselling contract with the child and the child must be informed.

Chapter 5
Talking About Disability

It is important for a number of reasons that children have accurate information, suited to their level of understanding, about their own disability or illness. For children attending a school where other children are disabled or any club, centre or hospital where they meet disabled peers (in other words, almost every child with a disability) it is also important that they have some understanding of other disabilities and illnesses.

Characteristic feelings about disability

Guilt

Guilt about being sick or disabled is experienced by many children. A nine-year-old boy expressed a common reasoning,

> 'I've got to be bad, see? Well, everyone knows if you do something bad you get punished. Well, being in a wheelchair is a punishment, you can't do things, that's a punishment. I'm being punished. I haven't *done* anything bad, not really bad, so I must be a bad person, right? And bad people have to be punished. So.'

Guilt is also experienced when children recognise that their parents are seen as objects of pity, or they overhear or are told of the problems they cause. Such phrases as, 'I don't know how you manage with him' are probably kindly meant but said in the presence of the child establish him as 'A Problem'. A mother sighing or complaining of exhaustion in the hearing of the child establishes a view of himself as a burden. A child described in another book (Brearley and Birchley, *Counselling in Disability and Illness* – See the Reading List at the back of this book.) echoed a remark she had obviously heard more than once when she described herself as being 'on her mother's back'.

Hospital and social services appointments often tend to concentrate on 'problems' and the child is confirmed in his perception of himself. He is a problem. It is his fault.

Fear

Fear is a common reaction due to lack of information. Children fear that their disability will worsen, even that they will die. With some conditions this may well be true and the child needs carefully and sensitively shared knowledge. However, many children with stable disabilities believe that they are ill and will die as they may have experienced another child's death.

A child whose parents regard him (unjustifiably) as fragile will experience fear. Sharon had spina bifida and was twelve when she developed epilepsy. Her parents were terrified by her occasional brief grand mal attacks and conveyed their fear. Sharon was convinced that she was an invalid and would soon die. Clear information provided to her and to her parents helped a little but the matter of fact approach of her school when either Sharon or one of her class had a fit was unfortunately counterbalanced by the extreme panic when her parents observed any signs that led them to anticipate a fit at home.

Anger

Anger can sometimes be more constructively used and directed when the child has an understanding of the causes of disability and illness. Charlie (see also Chapter 8), a six-year-old with cerebral palsy, was angry with his mother because he thought she had failed to prevent him becoming disabled. He thought she had been busy when it was decided! He also felt very confused and unhappy about his feelings as he loved his mother very much. A talk between Charlie, his mother and the counsellor about cerebral palsy – and Charlie's feelings – led to a real understanding and the revelation to Charlie that his mother also felt angry about his disability. A discussion about what to do with the anger led to some suggestions about expressing it and a lot of shared laughter.

Power

Power over prejudice and slights encountered by the child with a disability can be conferred by knowledge. Laurel was able to respond to a jeer of 'spastic!' from neighbour's children with the information that her disability was in fact spina bifida, not cerebral palsy and was much comforted by being able to educate them. Children also enjoy the surprise of adults when they can respond to queries about their disability with a short lecture on the cause and effect of their condition.

Reassurance

Reassurance about hidden fears or perceived inadequacies is often much needed. Sandra was philosophical about the physical effects of spina bifida but at fourteen was humiliated by her inability to read. She referred to herself as 'thick' and 'a real dumbo'. She would avoid having to read anything and had a large repertoire of excuses and evasions to achieve this. When it was explained that perceptual problems were often associated with spina bifida and hydrocephalus and the results of this were demonstrated she was fascinated. She would explain this to visitors to her school and show them the test materials, comparing her responses to theirs. An unexpected result was that with her extra confidence she started to try to read – and achieved a reading age of eight years by the time she was fifteen.

The first lesson of a group course in disability and illness

Whenever possible, teaching children about disability is most effective in a group with the chance for individual sessions after the lesson if a child wants to discuss a specific matter. The transcript of part of such a course follows to demonstrate the method used with a group of ten- to twelve-year-old children with a range of disabilities and varying learning levels.

No child is asked a question directly but all answers offered are respected and discussed. In this group one of the children was happy to be used as an example and enjoyed the attention of her peers. If this is not appropriate in a particular group for any reason then an imaginary child can be described. The answers recorded are those given by one specific group. The children's comments are given in italics.

The course would extend over several sessions with time allowed for questions and comments – and careful observation and listening.

The lesson

'Everyone in the world is special.
Everyone in this room is special.
Everyone in the world is different: even identical twins are different.
Everyone in this room is different. For example: I am tall, Katie is short.
Can you tell me any ways in which people are different?'
'Fat and thin.'
'My gran is old and my sister is young.'
'Curly hair and straight hair.'
'Different colour skin.'
'Happy people and miserable people.'
'Wheelchairs and walkers.'

'Yes, lots of differences. What about the last one? I thought wheelchairs and walkers were things, not people?'
'Oh, you know – handicapped and not.'
'What people can do, you know, running and so on.'
'Yes, and talkers and not talkers.'

'Right! So, one of the things that is different is that some people are disabled and some are not. Why is that?'
'Born like it.'
'Not everyone – some people get hurt or get ill or something, then they are handicapped.'

'So it isn't their fault – that they are disabled?'
'No, of course it isn't.'
'Could be, if they ran into the road and got hit by a car.'
'Yes, but that's really an accident, you can't blame a child.'
'Well, if they're born like that it isn't their fault.'
'Whose fault is it, then?'
'The doctor? You can't always blame the doctor.'

'So there are different sorts of disability and we are not sure always

what causes disability. Do you know the names of any disabilities?'
'I think its called spastic.'
'Spinal bifida or something, that's what I've got.'
'Fits.'
'Not being able to walk.'
'My nan's blind now.'
'Some people are mental.'
'That's mentally handicapped. They do baby things.'
'Danny died last year. He had muscle something.'

'Right – a lot of names. Before we talk about them it will help to know a bit about how our bodies work. What things can our bodies do?'
'Move round – walk, run.'
'Not everyone, people in wheelchairs can't walk.'
'They can move, move their arms and things.'

'Right, so people can move...'
'And talk – well, or Bliss or sign or something.'
'Communicate.'
'Everyone can make a noise, anyway.'

'What are you all doing now – as well as communicating?'
'Listening.'
'Fidgeting – well, Dean is!'
'Thinking.'

'Right! So we can move, communicate, think, feel and lots of other things. What part of our body is in charge of all these things – who's the Big Boss?'
'Up here.' (tapping head)
'Your heart?'
'Your head.'

'Your heart is very important and you couldn't live without it: but yes, your head, or what is inside your head.'
'Your brain.'
'He hasn't got a brain.'

'He has a good working brain like everyone else – it told him what you said to him and told his muscles to make his arm push you – and now it's telling his face and breathing muscles to laugh! Your brain is

the Boss, the one in charge. Right. If the Headteacher wanted to tell
me something and I was teaching, what could he do?'
'Come down and tell you.'
'Leave you a note.'
'Wait until break and tell you then.'
'Telephone you.'
'Send one of the kids to say he wanted you.'
'No – send a kid with a note.'
'Shout!'

'Yes, he could do all those things. Let's talk about him sending a
message. The Boss wants to send a message to a teacher and he can't
leave his room. So he sends a message by telephone.

    Your brain wants to send a message to your foot but it can't leave
your head. So – it sends a message by telephone, or something
similar.

    If a message has got to get from your brain to your foot – maybe if
Dan's brain wants to tell his foot to stop kicking the table – oh! it
did! He's stopped! Now – how did Dan's brain do that?'
*'Telephoned his foot! Hello, foot, Miss is getting ratty 'cause you're
kicking the table!'*

'You're nearly right. Actually, the bit about me getting ratty is
happening in the *thinking* part of his brain. The message to the foot
was to the muscles of his foot and said, 'Keep still'. If I told you the
message went along a tiny thread all the way from his brain to his
foot, could you tell me the name of that thread? You have them all
over your body.'
'Veins.'
'Blood vessels.'
'Skin.'

'Yes, all those things go all over your body but they have other jobs.'
'Give us a clue!'
'What's the letter?'

'Right – it starts with N.'
'N-n-n...'
'Neck?'
'No, silly, all over. N-n-n...'
'Nerves?'

'Well done – yes, nerves. Nerves go from the back of your brain all over your body. [Shows a simple diagram of the brain and nervous system – see Fig. 5.1]. So – starting here, in this place in the brain, the message starts as a tiny electric current, like a telephone wire, down the nerve inside the backbone, right down here, then out down the leg until it reaches the muscle, here. There is a special place in the brain that looks after movement, tells the muscles what to do, and a special nerve that carries the message all the way. It is close together with lots of other nerves in the backbone – the spinal cord, here. Hundreds of nerves all going to all the parts of the body.

Messages can go the other way, too. Suppose I tickle Sally's hand?'

'*Ouch.*'

Fig. 5.1 Simplified diagram of the brain and nervous system used in teaching children about disability.

'I don't think it hurt – but you did feel it. So what happened there?'
'Your brain told your hand to tickle her.'
'Yes, and your mouth said what you were going to do.'

'Yes, and my brain told my mouth what to say. But what happened when Sally said "Ouch!"?'
'It hurt!'
'No it didn't.'

'How did Sally know I had touched her? She wasn't looking.'
'She felt it.'
'She felt it and a message went to her brain.'
'And then her brain went ouch!'
'Told her mouth to go ouch!'

'Well done. Now – let's look at what happens when someone's muscles don't move when the person wants them to. Jo – can we talk about you? Thank you. Jo has cerebral palsy – right, Jo? And her legs won't move when she wants them to. Why not?

Jo, can your brain decide you want to move? Yes. So the Boss is there. The Boss understands what is going on. There is nothing wrong with the thinking part.

Can you feel if I touch your foot, Jo? Yes – so the message is going up from Jo's foot to her brain – the nerve is OK. And Jo's legs move about so the muscles are working.

When Jo was a tiny baby inside her mother – before she was born, the part of her brain that is in charge of sending messages to her muscles got damaged.'
'How?'
'What happened?'

'No one knows. It wasn't anything anyone did – and it wasn't anything anyone didn't do. No one's fault. No one's decision – nobody made it happen.'
'Just one of those things.'

'Exactly. So, when little baby Jo started to want to move, her brain knew what it wanted to do but the message sending bit wouldn't work.'
Jo: (using Bliss) Why no speak?

'Exactly the same reason. We use – well, who can guess how many muscles we use to speak?'
'Three?'
'About ten.'
'One or two.'

'If you think about it, watch me talking. I have to breathe – that takes muscles. Then I have to move my lips, my tongue, my cheeks – so it's about a hundred muscles, all having to move together at the right time to make all the different sounds. All those messages at the same time – and the message part of the brain not working.

The thinking and feeling and learning parts of the brain are all working fine ...'
'And the seeing and the hearing ...'
'That's her eyes and ears, silly.'
'Yes but it goes to her brain, doesn't it?'
'Like messages again.'

'Right, yes. All that working, but the message sending part not working.'
'What about spina bifida?'
'We will talk about that – that's a different story. We'll talk about other disabilities as well so that we can understand all of them.'

Children who do not have accurate information about their disability can experience feelings of guilt about being disabled, fear about symptoms they do not understand, fear about dying, and anger. Knowledge can give power and reassurance.

Teaching needs to include clear and accurate information about the working of the human body as well as the causes and effects of damage and illness. Teaching in a group is effective and gives opportunity for discussion and example. The use of simple pictures and diagrams can be very effective.

Chapter 6
Bereavement

There are a number of models used in studies of the effects of disability. One of these models has been found particularly useful as a source of insight and understanding into counselling children with special needs.

The bereavement model

As mentioned in Chapter 1, the model for considering the emotional needs of children with disability and illness is that of bereavement. Bereavement is the experience of loss and deprivation usually described in relation to someone experiencing loss by the death of a person close to them.

Bereavement results in mourning and the bereaved person experiences a number of different emotions and reactions. Someone who is bereaved goes through a number of stages of mourning. Not everyone experiences all the stages and there is no particular order in which they are experienced. When the mourner is able to enjoy what is for him an acceptable life then resolution is said to have occurred.

There is no time limit for working through each stage and resolution may be achieved in time or may appear to have been achieved but an anniversary, stress or an incident recalling the bereavement may cause a recrudescence of feelings.

The stages of bereavement are as follows:

- Denial
- Anger
- Guilt
- Grief
- Depression.

Denial is often the first reaction to news of loss. The exclamation 'Oh, no!' is a common immediate reaction, and the recipient may continue to deny consciously what has happened.

Denial at a deeper level occurs when the person seems unable to take in what he is told. He will mishear or interpret what he is told as meaning that the loss has not occurred. He may insist on unrealistic hope or may refuse to discuss the matter.

Anger is a very common but often the least acceptable aspect of bereavement. Anger may be directed at the person who has died for going away, for not saying goodbye or for causing the accident or illness that was the cause of death. Anger may be directed at a person who can in some way be blamed for the death. The bereaved person may feel deep anger at other people who have not been bereaved. As anger is seldom acceptable, it may be suppressed or misdirected.

Guilt is a very painful emotion. The bereaved person may feel guilty because he expressed anger towards the dead person or he forgot or omitted some action and this might have hurt the one whom he has lost. He may feel guilt because he imagines he has in some way caused the death, either by action, omission or wish. If he can find no obvious cause he may search for obscure sins on his part.

Grief or sorrow is expected of a bereaved person and he will usually be allowed to grieve openly. It is not always possible for sorrow to be expressed. There may be responsibilities that need to be undertaken or arrangements made. Other people may have to be supported. Social expectations may make weeping unacceptable – for example, the accepted wisdom that 'men don't cry' makes it very difficult for many men to shed tears. Other people may be embarrassed or impatient of tears and 'bravery' held up as an admirable trait.

Grief may be suppressed and denied, sometimes diverted to anger, guilt or depression. The grief may be so deep that the mourner is afraid of expressing it, feeling he will go mad or never be able to stop grieving.

Depression, when the bereaved person becomes overwhelmed by the situation and becomes unable to function or express any emotion, may result from suppressed anger or unexpressed grief. It can also be symptomatic of unworked-through stages in mourning, the depressed person being 'stuck' and unable to progress in the process of mourning.

Any of these stages can engender fear. There may be fear of hearing worse news or having to hear what is being denied. Anger is a common cause of fear, fear of losing control, of being seen as a bad person, fear of hurting another person, fear of rejection. Guilt carries the fear of discovery and punishment. Grief, as has already been mentioned, carries the fear of being overwhelmed and destroyed. Depression is in itself a very frightening condition when everything seems out of control and hopeless.

Bereavement and disability

The process described has been associated with death, but there are other forms of bereavement. Disability is one of these.

The child born with a disability has been bereaved of experiences, abilities and the opportunity to learn in the same way as his able peers. He is often bereaved of contact with other children, of mainstream education and of being accepted into his community on the same terms as his peers. He may be bereaved of self-esteem, hopes and expectations of the future and a good self-image. He has been bereaved of whatever is normality in his family and community. He has often been bereaved of respect and consideration regarding his right to privacy. He has been bereaved of independence.

The child who has acquired disability due to illness or accident has been bereaved of all these things and of the person he was before the illness or accident.

Children's comments on the stages of bereavement

Children have commented on their feelings about disability in terms that indicate that the process of mourning a bereavement is relevant to disability.

Denial

'I can do anything I want to, I just don't want to.'
'I would be able to do those things if I had gone to a normal school.'
'I can read if I want to but it is boring.'
'If I had an operation I could walk, I wouldn't need a wheelchair.'

Anger

'It's someone's fault I am disabled [doctor or midwife, mum or dad, God].'
'I'm stupid because I can't do things.'
'People are stupid, they don't listen, they don't try to understand me.'
'Why me? Why should I be disabled? What have I ever done?'
'I hate my brother, he can walk and he's only two.'

Guilt

'Dad left because I'm disabled.'
'It's because she's got me on her back mum got ill.'
'I have bad feelings, I'm a bad person, that's why I don't get better.'
'I'm jealous of other children who can do things, I sometimes wish bad things would happen to them, I'm a really horrible person.'

Grief

'Why can't I do things? I wish I could walk, I wish I wasn't handicapped.'
'I don't want to have to have a wheelchair.'
'I wish I wasn't me.'

Depression

'I'm ugly, no-one ever wants to be my friend.'
'If I go out in the park all the kids call me names so I stay in my bedroom.'
'It doesn't matter what anyone does, I'm not going to get better so why bother.'

Richard was a young teenager going through the bereavement of an almost total acquired disability and the knowledge of his own impending death.

The first message in his recently acquired communication system that related to his situation was, 'Question afraid to die hurt alone'. He was afraid to die, fearful that it would involve pain and that he would be alone when he died. The counsellor acknowledged both his fear and her inability to make any promises or predictions. She did share her own experiences of the deaths of three close relatives where death was not apparently painful and where the dying person had been with someone who loved them. She talked about hospices and pain control.

Richard returned to this subject many times in the next year but seemed calm and relaxed during subsequent discussions about the possible nature of his death. He asked the counsellor to tell his parents that he knew he was going to die and to ask them to talk to him. This was difficult as the parents were certain that Richard had no idea of his condition and they themselves refused to discuss him with staff. The counsellor decided that her responsibility was to Richard and talked to the parents. They were very distressed that Richard was aware (he had heard his case being discussed when apparently in a coma) and his mother felt unable to talk to him. His father agreed to see Richard with the counsellor and tried to reassure him. Richard was not entirely happy with the outcome but accepted that in this instance he might be stronger than his mother and father and more able to think about his dying. Richard decided to write a letter to his family and asked the counsellor to give it to them when she felt the time was right. The letter started, 'Thank you for happy for sad for love for anger.'

Richard asked if the counsellor knew anyone who had experienced the death of someone they loved. He wanted to talk to someone with that experience. Religion was important to Richard and the counsellor knew a woman of the same faith whose husband had died the previous year. She agreed to talk to Richard with the counsellor supporting and interpreting for Richard. She started by describing her husband's death, their last conversations and her feelings at the time and at present. Richard asked, 'question he angry'. She told him that yes, they had both been angry when they thought about everything that they would no longer do together and she still sometimes felt angry. Richard asked 'who' and she responded, 'Oh, everybody – I was angry with him for leaving me, he was angry with me for being left behind, we were both angry with God...' Richard was urgently signalling 'yes' and his visitor told him that she thought it would be much worse for him because he was at the start of his life. She asked if he ever felt angry and he responded with a very strong 'yes'. This was the first time he had communicated that he was feeling anger.

Richard began to express his anger and sadness, screaming and sobbing as he worked through his painful emotions, repeating 'angry sad angry'.

Richard started wanting to communicate his situation and feelings to other people and received a lot of support from his peers. One striking example of this is described in Chapter 12. Richard seemed to know intuitively that he needed to acknowledge the emotions of mourning first with the counsellor and then with other people. He expressed his fears, grief, anger and guilt. In his last year although his physical condition deteriorated Richard was calm and relaxed, joining in the activities of his group when he was able, revealing an impish sense of humour. He seemed to have reached a resolution and his death when it came was quiet and peaceful.

Richard was experiencing bereavement connected with his own death. Children who are ill and disabled can experience the stages of bereavement relating to their impairments.

In the next five chapters we will look at the emotional problems of children with disability in the terms of each stage of bereavement briefly previewed here and at some techniques for enabling them to work through their feelings and in some cases achieve resolution.

The names and some of the details of the children described have been changed to preserve anonymity but their words and the details of the counselling described are accurate.

Chapter 7
Denial

Denial is the conscious or subconscious refusal to acknowledge a fact. In the case of a death it is easy to recognise when a bereaved person is denying the reality of that death. In the case of disability or illness it can be less obvious that denial is occurring. The disabled person may not be aware of the implications of his disability. With an acquired disability he may be so shocked by this that he is unable to hear or understand what he is told about that disability. A child may not understand the ways in which disability may affect his life. He may have limited experience or understanding of life outside his immediate family and special school. In none of these cases would 'denial' be an appropriate description of an inability to be realistic about expectations and limitations.

However, denial can and does occur. Denial by a child can be the result of a number of different causes.

Family influences

The influence of the family is very significant in the life of any child. When that child is dependent for longer than average, the family influence is reinforced. Additionally many families with a child who is ill or disabled are socially isolated. Time is limited by the need for care, problems of mobility restrict outings, feelings of embarrassment or the problem of having to explain and answer questions can impose isolation. If the disabled child is the only one of school age and travels by school bus to a distant special needs school, the social contact with other local families may be lost. Isolated in this way the child has little opportunity for comparison with able peers or an awareness of how much more support he is receiving than other children.

Some parents may be unable or unwilling to recognise the effects of disability or wish to protect their child from hurt and distress. Their perception of their child's disability or their decision to protect their child can lead to very unrealistic hopes and expectations. Paul's parents had always told him that 'one day' he would have an operation and would be able to walk, run and play football. Paul was almost totally paralysed from a high-level spina bifida and at eleven years old was asking with increasing desperation when such an operation was going to be performed. He rejected any explanations from teachers, doctor and counsellor. He knew – mum and dad had told him.

Others' expectations

Children may also be given unrealistic expectations by other people.

Salim told everyone that he was going to join the army when he grew up. He was severely restricted after head injury with strength, balance and coordination so impaired that he needed an electric wheelchair. Even when he was sixteen many people were responding to his stated ambition with such comments as, 'That sounds exciting,' 'Will you be an officer?'

It can be argued that everyone needs hope and that it is cruel and unfeeling to deny a child hope. The question that should be considered is that of the damage done when an unrealistic hope is eventually and inevitably dashed. To help a child, sensitively and supportively, to distinguish between unattainable dreams and possible hopes is neither cruel nor unfeeling but positive and constructive. It is helpful to start by using an amusing example from the counsellor's own experience to clarify the difference between dreams and hopes. Most children will appreciate the humour of being told that their middle-aged, very tall and overweight counsellor cherished dreams of being a ballet dancer and will realise that a realistic hope for her would be learning ballroom dancing. Making a drawing of, writing or talking about 'my dreams' and 'my hopes' can lead to useful discussion about what goes into each category and why.

The above examples may seem to be denial. Unattainable dreams and unrealistic hopes may presage true denial but may be due more to lack of information or adult collusion than denial. True denial, though, can and does occur. To the child, there are advantages in denial. A child who denies that he cannot walk ('I just don't want to') not only does not have to work at compensatory skills, but also does not have to face up to life as a wheelchair user. Karol refused physiotherapy to help him use callipers and walking aids, insisting that he could walk perfectly well. Challenged to demonstrate he placidly replied that he would – tomorrow. Sheila claimed many achievements that were patently impossible, these always occurring at home or on holiday. She did not need to learn to read because she had read the lesson in church, a long piece from the Bible. She did not need to practice typing because she spent the holiday working as a typist in her father's office, doing all his correspondence. As the fantasy of a four-year-old this might just be acceptable but Sheila was fourteen. Unable to cope with her limitations she denied all of them and with that denial was unable to develop the skills and abilities that she did have.

Counselling in denial

When denial is disadvantaging the child, intervention in the form of counselling can be helpful. Building up the child's self-esteem and working towards a positive self-image must of course be the aim of all his activities but the counsellor's help is often needed in initiating and supporting this and in suggesting strategies. Concentrating on the child's abilities and skills should accompany a gentle acknowledgement of the reality of his disability. Knowledge of the causes and effects of disability is important (see Chapter 5). Meeting adults with similar disabilities will help understanding of the positive aspects of life as a disabled person, as also will suitable videos and books. Older children can gain greatly from identifying social handicaps (discrimination, access problems, denial of rights) and campaigning for improvements.

The counsellor must at the same time recognise and accept the pain, anger and grief the child may be experiencing. It is not helpful to respond with such phrases as 'I know how you feel'. Unless the counsellor herself has experienced severely restricting disability she cannot possibly 'know' how it feels. She can try to understand by listening and enabling the child to express his feelings and by acknowledging the validity of such feelings. To say, 'I cannot imagine how bad it feels, I cannot imagine how I would feel but I do understand the feelings you are talking about and I do understand why you feel like that' may seem inadequate. To a child who has usually been responded to with meaningless reassurance or attempted distraction it can be releasing and affirming.

Hannah was nine years old, severely disabled and non-verbal as a result of athetoid cerebral palsy. She seemed a cheerful, placid child with a ready chuckle and alert expression. Her attitude to anything requiring effort was described as 'extremely laid-back' and although apparently quite intelligent she was seriously underachieving, making no progress in school either intellectually or physically. Counselling was requested.

Initially Hannah gave no indication that everything was not happy in her perception of her world. Identifying her feelings from a selection of labelled faces [see Fig.7.1] she selected 'happy'. Asked if there were any other feelings she smiled and shook her head. Choosing from pieces of coloured silk she selected a bright pink and clearly enjoyed being swathed in this, wheelchair and all. Asked to indicate a stone from a collection of stones and pebbles she chose a smooth, polished piece of turquoise and described it as 'beautiful' and 'happy'. (Descriptions of these techniques will be found in Chapter 12.) It was with the introduction of 'Jemima', a large rag doll, that Hannah moved from her stance. Jemima was seated in a buggy, wore Piedro boots and had a Bliss communication book. The counsellor said, 'Hannah, I have a puzzle for you to solve. Jemima is not feeling happy. She is a new Bliss user and cannot think how to tell me what is wrong. I want you to help. Can you imagine why she is not happy?' Hannah was enthusiastic. She communicated strongly and clearly, 'no talk no walk'.

In the dialogue that follows the counsellor's words are in standard type, Hannah's symbol communication in italic.

'Are you saying that Jemima can't talk or walk?'
'Yes. Wheelchair.'
'Jemima is in a wheelchair and she can't walk or talk.'
'No Bliss.'
'No, she has only just got her Bliss book.'
'Sad.'
'Who is sad?'
'Me. Girl.'

'You and Jemima are sad?'
'Girl sad.'
'Jemima is sad. You also gave me the symbol "me". Did I make a mistake?'
'Me sad girl.'
'I see – you are sad for Jemima, sorry for Jemima. Yes, I feel very sorry that Jemima feels so sad. Do you know why she is so sad?'
'Sad wheelchair.'
'Do you mean wheelchair, I wonder – or are you using that symbol for something else? Hannah, are you saying that Jemima is sad because she is disabled?'
'Yes.' (emphatically)
'So, Jemima feels sad because she is disabled. Poor Jemima. Does she have any other difficult feelings, I wonder?'
'Angry upset.'
'She feels angry and upset too. I can understand that – it must be very difficult for Jemima, wanting to do things and not being able to. It must be sad and frustrating for her. She must want to cry sometimes.'
'Hit.'
'And hit people, yes. Very angry feelings.'
'Hug.'
'You want to hug Jemima – show her you understand? You understand how she feels?'
'Yes I feel.'
'Are you saying that you sometimes feel like Jemima? Sad and angry and frustrated? Well, that's not surprising. Perhaps it might help next time you feel like that if you tell about it and then you can get a hug as well, like Jemima.'
'We me girl.'
'Yes, you and Jemima, feeling the same and needing a hug. Both.'

Clearly, Hannah knew very well the feelings she attributed to the doll. She appeared to feel safe describing the doll's feelings. When the counsellor showed that she understood and accepted those feelings Hannah was able to own her own feelings.

Kevin was involved in a serious accident when he was ten years old which resulted in the amputation of one arm and almost no

Fig. 7.1 Drawings of faces (reduced in size) showing a range of emotions. These may be used as appropriate, the child being offered selected faces or asked to choose from the whole range. The counsellor may need to read and, if necessary, explain the emotions illustrated.

Fig. 7.1 *Contd.*

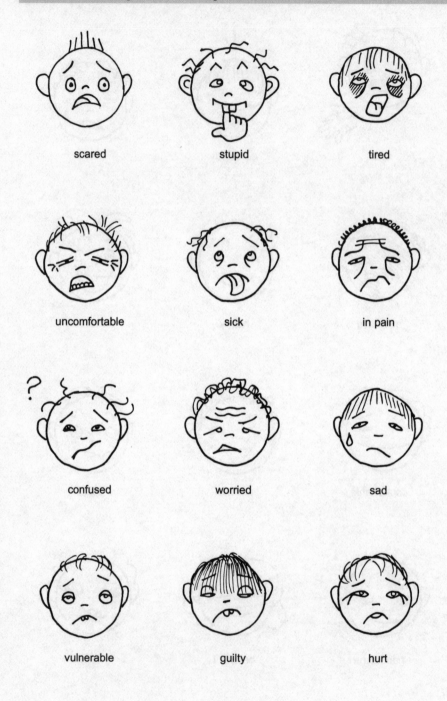

Fig. 7.1 Contd.

confident   helpless   indifferent

picked on   love   hate

Fig. 7.1 *Contd.*

function in the other. A very physically strong boy he was unable to accept any of the limitations of his disability and fought everyone who attempted to help him. He was resentful of help that he had to accept. Kevin was extremely difficult to contain in school, fighting and boasting continually of imagined feats and running away when things got difficult.

On one occasion the counsellor was the only adult near when Kevin violently attacked a younger boy. She had to physically restrain him to protect the other boy and held Kevin tightly in spite of him kicking, biting and swearing. It was a battle of strength which she felt she had to win. Kevin suddenly went limp and collapsed on the ground sobbing bitterly. He allowed her to help him to his feet and take him to the counselling room where she made him a cup of coffee and gave him a box of tissues. She sat quietly until he was calm.

'Are you going to send me to the Head?'
'No.'
'Why not?'

'I would prefer to talk to you myself.'

'Why?'

'Because I don't feel that you are very happy fighting everyone.'

'Well, I can beat anyone, I'm really strong.'

'Yes, you are. Physically.'

'What? What do you mean?'

'Just what I say. I think you are physically very strong – but –'

'But what?'

'But not yet strong enough inside to manage what has happened to you.'

'Am so.'

'So why are you fighting everybody? Even little boys like David?'

'Don't know.'

'Perhaps you do know. Kevin, you know I am a counsellor? That means that I am used to helping people talk about really difficult things and keeping quiet about what they tell me.'

'Secrets, you mean?'

'Yes, secrets. I would only tell if it was a bad secret – like, someone was being hurt or abused. Then I would need to tell someone – or help you tell.'

'There's nothing like that.'

'OK.'

'It's just – it's – well, they can do everything, they've got hands and everything, I can't do nothing. It's not fair. I wish I was dead and then I wouldn't have to see them all the time.'

It took a violent episode where his feelings were very strong and he was physically frustrated from doing what he later said he hated doing – fighting other children – for Kevin to admit his feelings about the devastating thing which had happened to him. In the rest of the session and in many which followed he poured out his feelings to the counsellor. He proved to have a great deal of insight in suggesting strategies by which he could manage those feelings. His ideas included permission to leave class and run round the playing fields when he felt 'like exploding' instead of running away or fighting, and to set his own punishments when he broke rules. These punishments were often very original and far harsher than any the school would have imposed. He carried out his self-imposed tasks cheerfully and used counselling to work through the feelings that had precipitated his outbursts.

Katie was thirteen and had to have a major operation to her spine and hips. She was accepting and cooperative through a number of painful procedures but when the operation was performed and she was in plaster in hospital she became very withdrawn and silent. She stopped eating and was slowly deteriorating to a very weak state. She continued to cooperate with the demands of her treatment and always whispered 'thank you' to the doctors and therapists. She insisted that nothing was wrong, she just wasn't very hungry, her back hurt a bit but it was alright.

She knew the counsellor well from earlier group sessions and agreed to talk with her.

'How are things with you, Katie?'

'Alright.'

'Everything is alright with you?'

(long silence)

'So you are fine.'

(started to cry quietly)

'Katie, you don't sound fine to me. You look very sad and you are crying.'

'... it hurts ... they said ... they said...'

'They said?'

'They said it wouldn't hurt, they all said...'

'Everyone told you it wouldn't hurt – and it hurts a lot?'

'It hurts – it was supposed to stop it hurting, it hurts worse.'

'So you were in pain, you were told an operation would stop the pain and you are still in a lot of pain? Have you asked about this?'

'No. They think ... they wanted ... it's supposed to be better.'

'They thought it would be better and you don't want to say it isn't?'

'My fault.'

'It's your fault it isn't better? How so?'

'I don't know.'

'So – you are in pain, feeling guilty, feeling...? I wonder. I think I would have other feelings if I had been told an operation would take the pain away and it wasn't true.'

'Doctors tell lies. Think I'm stupid.'

'Don't think you are able to understand the truth. You want to know the truth. OK. Do you want me to tell you the truth?'
(starting to cry again)
'Scary? It's your choice.'
'*Yes.*'
'OK. Katie, I think that the doctors were not telling you lies, they perhaps were not thinking carefully enough to explain everything. The operation went well, but it is a big operation and a lot of muscles and nerves had to be cut and moved around. That leaves a lot of swelling and bruising and a lot of pain. That pain will get better – if you are keeping strong and fit.'
'*They should have told me. They didn't tell me.*'
'You sound angry about that.'
'*Ye-e-s. Maybe a bit.*'
'Just a bit angry. So what is the bigger bit of feeling?'
'*A lot angry. And afraid.*'
'Tell me about the afraid.'
'*Well – if it hurt more – I mean, it was supposed to be better.*'
'It was supposed to be better but it hurt a lot more – and you were afraid.'
'*Well, I thought if it was worse, if I wasn't going to get better – well, you know.*'
'Perhaps I do. Can you find the word – the word that is so frightening?'
(in a whisper) '*Die.*'
'You thought you might die. And that was so frightening you couldn't say it to anyone.'
'*I thought – if I didn't actually say it – if I tried not to think it . . .*'
'It might not happen. That sounds a very difficult thing to do – like real hard work. Not saying, trying not to think.'
'*Yes.*'
'Katie, the nurse is bringing tea. When we have had a cup, perhaps you can decide what you want to do about all this anger, fear and hard work hiding it. OK?'
'*OK. Yes – OK.*'

Katie's attempted denial of her feelings and the conflict of feelings was consuming all her energy. She felt anger with the doctors, guilt at that feeling, wanting to please (perhaps feeling it would be risky not to please people who had a great deal of power over her) but resenting what she perceived as demands to be cooperative and grateful, and above all intense fear. When she had admitted her feelings she had begun resolution. With the help of the counsellor she talked to her doctor and received a clear explanation of the surgery and the process of healing. She was reassured that her feelings were acceptable and was encouraged to express them. She began to eat again and slowly gained strength and energy.

Looking at some examples of children in denial may help the reader identify when this is happening with other disabled children. What many cases have in common is the collusion of the adults. A child who is denying the reality of his situation is hiding or suppressing feelings that adults would find difficult or disturbing. It can be more comfortable to believe that the child is happy, doesn't understand or has come to 'accept' the consequences and limitations of his illness or disability.

A child who does not appear to complain or express frustration, anger or fear may be signalling his distress in other ways. Aggressive or tearful outbursts, clinging behaviour, phobias, eating problems, can all signal unexpressed fear and anger. The counsellor who offers permission to express the real feelings a child is experiencing can offer that child relief and reassurance.

Chapter 8
Anger

Anger is conventionally perceived by adults as well as by children as being a bad or a negative emotion. It is perceived as destructive, wicked, a failure. To feel anger, however justified, is wrong.

This attitude supposes that we have control over our feelings, that we can make a conscious decision not to feel a particular emotion. This is an error; we feel what we feel. It is important that any child is given the message that feelings are natural. It is what we *do* with feelings that is important.

Denial of anger

Denial of the validity of feelings and the delegation of some feelings as bad or negative can lead to the suppression of these feelings. To deny our feelings, to pretend we do not experience them, is very difficult. It can take a great deal of our energy. Children who learn that some feelings are not acceptable can learn at a very early age to deny or suppress these feelings. They may relieve the tension of anger by crying. They may display disruptive or aggressive behaviour, phobias, depression or self-destructive behaviour such as biting themselves. A child who has strongly negative feelings about anger will become afraid of his own feelings and afraid of anger in other people.

Adults may have their own problems with anger and pass these problems on to their own children, consciously or subconsciously. They may doubt their own ability to cope with anger and suppress any expression of anger in the child. They may be afraid of the implications of a child being angry about his disability.

Denny was the only child of a mother who was very afraid of anger after a restrictive upbringing and marriage to a violent husband. Denny was disabled with cerebral palsy and hydrocephalus. Determined that her son should not 'turn out like his dad' she taught him from an early age that anger was not allowed and dangerous. She always spoke softly, her manner was placatory and she coaxed and rewarded Denny into 'good' behaviour. Denny responded by becoming a submissive and timid child, terrified of other children and anxious always to be seen as good. He assured everyone that he didn't mind his disability. Denny was very attached to his mother and wept frantically when she moved out of sight. He took a long time to settle in school and wept every morning.

At the age of nine Denny started biting his arms and fingers, bruising and drawing blood. That, combined with his acute separation anxiety, prompted his school eventually to refer him for counselling four years later.

Offered pictures of faces expressing a number of emotions (see Fig. 7.1) Denny very apprehensively chose 'afraid'. With plenty of praise and reassurance from the counsellor he whispered that he was afraid of lots of things – his mother going away and never coming back, fire, being run over, getting cancer, vomiting, falling out of his wheelchair, dying in the night – the list seemed endless. When the counsellor asked if there was anything in school he was afraid of he said no – with a furtive, sideways look. She rephrased her question – was there anyone he was afraid of? Denny whispered the name of one teacher. Asked why this teacher frightened him he said, 'She shouts'. The counsellor offered the pictures again. 'Is there a face that reminds you of that teacher?' Denny bit his arm fiercely, chewed his fingers and averted his face, looking at the pictures sideways. After a time, he slowly extended a finger and jabbed it at the 'angry' face, pulling it back quickly.

It took many sessions before Denny felt able to confide that he often felt very angry and he was convinced that he was wicked and abnormal to experience such feelings. He was eventually able to identify the sources of his anger.

They included his father for deserting him, his mother for allowing the desertion, his disability and his isolation which he identified as 'me being so stupid that no-one likes me'.

Once Denny was able to accept that he was not wicked or

abnormal to feel anger and was encouraged to express his feelings and manage the anger he began the long progress towards healing. Enabled to express his anger, the fears became manageable. With the involvement of his mother in some counselling sessions and the cooperation of the school he eventually achieved a supported place at a mainstream college. He was successful in his courses and was planning for independent life in his own home with personal assistants.

The expression of anger

Helping children who have difficulties with anger involves a number of stages.

- The child needs the information that anger is a normal and common feeling and that people who feel angry are not wicked.
- The child needs to know that he will not be destroyed by his anger, neither can his anger destroy other people.
- He will need enabling to identify his feelings (use of pictures, dolls, stones, colours and other strategies are described in Chapter 12).

Safe ways of expressing anger can be suggested, with the counsellor accepting responsibility and control. Instead of words, actions can be very liberating.

Meggie was very severely disabled and non-verbal. She was able to make uncontrolled movements with one arm. On one occasion when Meggie was screaming and tense with anger the counsellor filled a metal waste paper bin with various small metal objects, placed it on Meggie's wheelchair tray and invited her to knock it onto the floor. The resultant crash represented violence for Meggie and she found it deeply satisfying and also very funny. After a triumphant shout and delighted giggling, she sighed deeply and relaxed completely. This activity was one she requested occasionally when feeling very tense.

Children who are able to may find writing or dictating a letter or poem describing how they feel helpful. Non-verbal children should have a private (and masked) set of symbols for words that may not be generally acceptable to use to express anger – although skilled users will find ways of doing this anyway. (The writer has encountered such ingenious constructions as 'not thinking old cow', 'sounds like kiss off' and 'farm rubbish'.)

Sometimes and most effectively it will be possible for the child with the support of the counsellor to express his anger to the person against whom his anger is directed.

A group of non-verbal children was invited to tell what made them angry. Charlie, aged six, (see Chapter 5) said that his friend made him angry when he took Charlie's toys. An older child said that she felt angry about being disabled and Charlie indicated strong agreement. Another child said that he sometimes got angry with his parents when they stopped him doing things. Charlie looked very surprised and when asked if he could say how he was feeling responded, 'why angry mum dad?' The teacher explained again what the other boy had said and asked Charlie if he was surprised that someone felt angry with their parents. Charlie said, 'yes'. He declined to say anything else in that session, looking very uncomfortable. The teacher asked him if he would like to talk to the counsellor about the session and he agreed.

With the counsellor, Charlie said that he felt he was bad because he felt angry with his mother. With much reassurance he told the counsellor that his anger was because she had let him be disabled. He thought that the doctor had asked if mum wanted a disabled baby and she, being very busy at the time, had said, 'yes, yes' without really listening. The counsellor explained about how Charlie's disability had been caused but Charlie was still worried. A meeting between Charlie, his mother and the counsellor was suggested and Charlie agreed.

The meeting was very successful. When the counsellor explained how Charlie was feeling his mother assured him that she, too, was angry that he was disabled. She did not want any other son than Charlie, she loved him and was proud of him, but she did wish that he was able to do the things he wanted to. Charlie was beaming and very satisfied.

Strategies for managing his own anger and that of other people need to be carefully worked out and practised. Denny was able to cope with a teacher he perceived as angry by imagining that she had come to class in her underwear and hadn't realised. Thus making her ridiculous, made him feel powerful and protected him against her anger. Pamela (Chapter 11) became interested in *why* other people became angry and exercising her insights exorcised her fear of their anger.

Harnessing anger

Quite young children are able to understand the concept that anger can make you strong and can be used to change things. Getting in touch with and experiencing their anger and then focussing it to reveal hidden strengths, is a very useful strategy for anyone and can be learned. A picture children often respond to, and one that makes use of common symbolism, is that of fire.

Fire as a symbol often appears in dreams and drawings and is usually an element of fear and horror. Fire is perceived as powerful and destructive. It rapidly gets out of control and consumes everything in its path. If it is hidden underground it will smoulder and eventually break out. The volcano is the ultimate symbol of the danger of fire, inevitably erupting in an inferno of total destruction.

Fire that is not controlled can burn and hurt. Fire that is controlled and used can keep us warm, cook our food, make things like pottery and drive machinery. In the same way that we can control and use fire, we can control and use our anger to give us courage, energy and assertion. Anger, like fire, will not destroy us or destroy others if we recognise it and use it appropriately.

Chapter 9

Guilt

Culture, religion and society

The concept of guilt is part of the morals of most cultures and religions. If there is a perception of a possible choice between right and wrong actions, then the concept of sin and guilt exists. There may be differing interpretations of choice and responsibility. Some religions, for example, subscribe to the belief that a child is born corrupt and must be taught moral behaviour (as in the doctrine of 'original sin') whereas others argue the innocence of the newborn child which must be protected. The child must be advised against the corrupting influence of the world. There may be a belief in universal standards of 'good' behaviour or there may be specific rules and strictures.

A child living in a society where there is a concept of guilt will be aware of an expectation that he will be 'good' as defined in his society, and be aware of rules for 'good' behaviour. This expectation will have been made clear to him by explanation, by punishment or disapproval of wrongdoing, by praise for doing right, depending on the customs of the society he grows up in or parental choice. He may learn that there are clear and consistent rules, or more likely that different situations demand different standards of behaviour. He may be confused by inconsistent or unclear expectations.

The existence of a conscience, whether as an inherent attribute that, in the words of Jiminy Cricket in Walt Disney's Pinocchio, can 'always be your guide', or as a taught and acquired sense, is usually considered desirable as a monitor of good and bad moral choice. A child who has done wrong and feels uncomfortable or afraid can be described as having a 'bad conscience'. He feels guilty. In this sense, guilt is seen as a good thing. The child is seen as having learnt that his behaviour is morally wrong.

For many of us, guilt is only appropriate when a deliberate choice has been made to do something accepted as wrong. Others feel that guilt is synonymous with the human condition. Those who have had conflicting moral education may be equally confused about feelings of guilt. Children who have been punished when they have not been aware of having done wrong may feel guilty all the time. However, where guilt is perceived as appropriate it will be seen as a 'good thing', a sign that the child has learned the difference between right and wrong.

It is more difficult to accept a child's feelings of guilt at being disabled.

Family problems

Some children do undoubtedly experience guilt because of their disability or because of its effects on other people. They know that they are 'a problem' and cause grief or difficulties for their families. They may well have the same difficulty as many other children in recognising where they do and do not have choice. How can a child who is incontinent not feel guilty when he sees that other children wetting or soiling themselves meet disapproval or are punished? How is he to distinguish between a parent's irritation with a dawdling sister and his own slow progress in walking? The word 'guilt' may not be in a child's vocabulary but he can express that he feels, or is, 'bad' or that problems are his 'fault'.

Choice and responsibility

Children trying to make sense of a world where things they experience as bad happen inexplicably, will find a convenient scapegoat in their own disability. Bad things happen, they reason, because they are disabled. It is their fault. Examples of such feelings are described in Chapter 5.

Katie, described in Chapter 7 – denial; Denny and Charlie in Chapter 8 – anger; all experienced guilt at feelings of anger. Anger is usually perceived as a 'bad' thing. Children who are disabled have many experiences and deprivations to feel angry about but rarely feel that anger is an acceptable reaction.

Other children say that the break-up of their parents' marriage or the illness or death of a family member are their fault, because they are disabled. They feel responsible and they feel guilty. One cause of such reasoning may well be limited experience of cause and effect. Most children develop a reasonable working model of their world where certain actions have predictable results. They learn by experience. In the words of the proverb, 'The burnt child fears the fire'. Such an extreme lesson, as well as many others, will be denied many children who are disabled. They are unable to explore their surroundings, discover the results of their actions. Able children begin at an early age to distinguish between preventable disasters and true accidents. Disabled children may be protected or physically prevented from such learning experiences. With limited opportunities for learning the cause and effect of their own actions, it is very difficult for the child to understand where he has choice and decision. He will be confused about situations where he must accept responsibility and what is beyond his control. He sees his disability causing problems and he feels responsible. He is bad. He feels guilty.

The counsellor must be aware that the child may well be right in his assessment of the effects of his disability on others. A marriage that is not strong may well disintegrate under the strains and demands of caring for a disabled child. Worry, fatigue and the physical stresses of handling a child who needs lifting and carrying may well result in illness or injury to the caring parent, especially when that parent is alone.

To deny this is to patronise the child. He will be very aware of strains, overhear remarks, even be directly blamed. What must be denied is that the child is guilty. A useful approach is to ask the child if he chose to be disabled? Did he decide not to be able to walk? Is it his fault that he needs help? Who asked him if he wanted to have a disability?

It then needs to be made clear that whatever happens is not his *fault* (unless he has chosen to be difficult, of course) and that he is probably the person that is most affected by his disability. Is he guilty because he makes himself frustrated? The silliness of this reasoning is usually apparent and makes the point.

A game of telling the stories of disasters and accidents, some clearly caused by careless or bad choices and others where no-one is to blame, and asking 'Whose fault?' and then, 'Who is guilty?' can emphasise the point.

It can also be helpful to explore with the child the circumstances that make difficulties in relationships. He needs to know that adults behave very much like children, they get tired and irritable, break friendships, say things they don't mean, are bad at saying sorry or explaining. For Charlie (Chapter 8), talking with his mother relieved his feelings of anger and guilt. If the child wants to tell his parents how he is feeling this may be very helpful. However, the risk that the parent may find the child's feelings difficult to accept should be discussed with the child first. The counsellor may be tempted to warn the parent in advance and prompt their response but others would feel that this would be a breach of confidence. The child can be asked if the counsellor may explain what the meeting is about in advance. His decision must be respected.

In the counselling relationship a great deal can be done to clarify areas of choice and responsibility. For example, the counsellor may have to cancel an appointment. How this is explained to the child is important.

- 'I am sorry that we could not meet yesterday. I was ill and had to stay in bed. I had no choice. I know you were disappointed but I hope you understand.' (The counsellor accepts responsibility for cancelling the appointment but explains that it was not her choice.)
- 'Yesterday I was asked to go to see John who is in hospital. I had to decide whether to go to the hospital or to see you. It was a difficult choice and I hope that you will understand. I am sorry I had to cancel our talk.' (The counsellor indicates clearly the choice she had to make and takes responsibility for her choice.)
- 'I have to apologise to you about yesterday. I forgot we had arranged to meet. I am very sorry, it was my fault for not writing it down. You must feel angry with me for not seeing you.' (The counsellor is at fault and acnowledges her responsibility.)
- 'I am angry that we could not meet yesterday. Transport was arranged but did not collect you. I have told the transport officer that I am angry about this. I am upset for you that you missed your appointment. It is important that people keep their promises.' (The cancellation was not the counsellor's responsibility. She places the blame and expresses her feelings.)

Having explained and identified responsibility where appropriate the child should be enabled to identify and express his feelings about the missed session. If the child expresses guilt (he may feel that he has upset the counsellor and she did not wish to see him or that he should not feel angry) the inappropriateness of this should be clarified.

With these and similar examples the child can be helped to distinguish between the concepts of choice and responsibility.

Chapter 10
Grief

The grieving child

For most people a weeping child evokes an almost reflex need to comfort. It is rewarding to identify the trouble, provide a solution and restore a smile. It is a common experience for the mother of a crying baby to be asked to hand the baby to every woman in the vicinity, all professing to be 'good with babies' and all with a special technique for stopping the crying. The one who is successful is usually flushed with pride and satisfaction.

Most children's tears are, after all, caused by easily solved problems. A broken toy can be mended or replaced, a bumped knee can be rubbed and soon forgotten, the child distracted from a disappointment or squabble. A treat, a joke, a present are all commonly used ploys to stop a child crying.

Sometimes the cause of a child's grief is not trivial. The causes of his grief are recognised by adults as significant. Adults can empathise with situations that would or do cause them great sadness. Examples are the death of a loved pet or grandparent, a painful injury or medical procedure, a promised treat or holiday cancelled, a friend's rejection or the cruelty of a bully. In these or similar situations the cause of the grief is usually recognised and acknowledged. The child will be allowed to weep and will receive comfort, cuddling and reassurance. Their right to grieve will be affirmed.

After what is judged a reasonable time, the child will be encouraged to stop grieving, to cheer up. He will be reasoned with ('Grandpa is gone, we all miss him but he wouldn't want you to be sad'). He is encouraged to symbolic actions ('We'll have a lovely funeral for Tibby and put a lovely bunch of flowers on his grave'). He will be reassured

('The pain will soon go away'). He will be offered an alternative ('We will go to Legoland® next week instead'). Action will be taken ('I will talk to Jason and sort this out.' 'I will come to school and make sure that this bullying stops'). The need to grieve has been acknowledged and the child's sadness accepted. In most cases it will be assumed that time, recompense or action will end the sadness. The child will then be expected to resume his usual happy life.

The disabled child

Children with special needs are often treated very differently. If a smile is not instantly forthcoming the child is rallied, 'Where's my nice cheerful sweetheart?' or teased, 'You'll curdle the milk with a face like that!' The child is exhorted to cheer up or greeted with a nickname such as 'smiler'. When he does respond with a smile he receives praise and affirmation. He may well overhear such remarks as, 'They're always so happy!' (a visitor to a special needs school) or 'Of course this is a very happy place' (staff showing a visitor round a respite care home). Such comments suggest that to appear happy is good and right and many children learn to wear a wide smile on almost every occasion.

When the child does cry a physical reason is usually suggested. He must be uncomfortable, need toiletting, have a pain. If the child is non-verbal he has less scope and is even less likely to be given the opportunity to express his feelings. The adult's need to solve the problem and make the child happy, makes perceived physical problems receive attention. The child is then jollied out of his tears. It is comparatively easy to elicit laughter from a child with athetosis. Thus his feelings are often trivialised in this way. Some adults are unable to cope with the idea that a child can experience the sort of pain they imagine they would feel in the same situation. They protect themselves by subconsciously denying any child's pain and refusing to allow any expression of it.

Expression of grief

When a child needs to express his grief and is enabled to, he can experience relief and affirmation.

Bobby established his own way of coping with grief. In a communication group he identified 'sad' as an emotion he experienced and related this to 'handicap'. As he talked about watching other able children he began to cry. He sobbed and howled for several minutes, the child next to him reaching out a sympathetic arm and others communicating their understanding and concern. When Bobby finished crying he gave several deep sighs and smiled at the group.

Subsequently at several month's interval, Bobby would say that he needed to cry. He would ask to lie on a beanbag and have a soft blanket over him. As the counsellor talked quietly about sad feelings he would begin to sob and would allow himself to break down completely for several minutes. These short sessions of experiencing and expressing his grief seemed to enable Bobby to cope effectively for the rest of the time.

Shane was a small, wiry boy of eleven with spina bifida. He was an accomplished wheelchair user, enjoying the dismay of visitors as he spun on one wheel or bumped his wheelchair down steps. Shane was, by his own admission, a 'tough' and seldom complained when a rough game of football with more able peers tipped him out of his chair and added another graze or bruise. Shane was a delight to teach, quick, enthusiastic and funny. He was well informed about his disability and matter-of-fact about his limitations. If he dismissed any possible problems related to his incontinence rather abruptly, this was easy to attribute to the natural reluctance of an eleven-year-old boy to discuss such matters.

On a school holiday with school mates and children from a mainstream school Shane was a great success. He was popular with his able peers who openly admired his acrobatic skills and attempted to emulate his tricks in borrowed wheelchairs. He showed sensitivity when an able room mate wet the bed and helped him change the sheets, saying that it happened to him sometimes, no problem.

One afternoon, a lively and good-natured battle developed between the boys, throwing pine cones at each other, taking cover behind tree trunks and making sorties for fresh supplies. Shane had abandoned his wheelchair and was scuttling on his hands when he suddenly burst into frantic sobbing. He turned to the counsellor who was sitting nearby and flung himself into her arms. The other boys gathered round, asking anxiously if he had hurt himself, but he shouted that he was alright. They moved away but stood nearby, shocked and concerned. Shane started to moan over and over again, 'It's not fair, it's not fair,' and when the counsellor asked, 'The other boys?' he nodded vehemently. She suggested, 'Why don't you tell them?' and he rather reluctantly agreed but insisted, 'You tell them instead.'

The counsellor called the other boys and explained to them that Shane was feeling very sad because they could all run and climb and he couldn't. They listened soberly and one said, 'I didn't realise you minded, Shane,' and the others agreed. One added, 'You're such a good athlete and everything, we didn't think the wheelchair mattered.' Shane listened and explained that he usually didn't care too much but sometimes when he got left behind or saw them doing easily what took him great effort or wasn't possible, he got upset. 'I usually hide it OK,' he added. One of the boys said wisely, 'I expect it's more difficult because we are here all the time and you get tired.'

One of the boys fetched Shane's wheelchair and they helped him in and went away, tactfully not pushing the chair. Shane was in high spirits for the rest of the evening. He did not refer to the matter again but did ask for the occasional counselling session when problems were worrying him.

Some children will cry frequently and often for no apparent reason or for trivial causes. They will ask for sympathy and attention by crying and may complain constantly of unkindness by other children or tell unlikely stories of injustice or lack of understanding. These are more likely to be signs of depression (see Chapter 11). Other causes of this apparent sadness could be repressed anger (see Chapter 8) or low self-esteem. All these are needs that can be met by counselling and the skilled counsellor should be able to help the child identify the causes of unhappiness.

Chapter 11
Depression

The term 'depression' is used for a very wide range of feelings from a vague 'I'm fed up' to the illness of clinical depression. For the purposes of this book, depression will be defined as a symptom of one or more of the following states: prolonged sadness, lack of hope, inability to experience enjoyment, withdrawal, feeling permanently unwell, lack of energy, tearfulness, eating disorders, irritability, indifference, obsessive habits.

Stresses for the disabled child

Children as young as three years have been observed to suffer from depression. Parents may describe the child as having appeared to 'give up' attempting to walk or crawl, that they 'can't be bothered' to talk or communicate. A previously outgoing child becomes unresponsive.

The causes of depression in so young a child can be difficult to discover. Initially it is important to look at the stresses the child is experiencing. It is often at the stage of emerging from babyhood to early childhood that the level of a child's disability becomes apparent. Able children are developing at a rapid rate:

- Having achieved walking skills they experiment with running, climbing, hopping and jumping.
- They are able to feed themselves, use cutlery, scribble and draw, manipulate toys, ride a tricycle.
- Their vocabulary increases enormously and they use language to direct their world and make choices.
- They become independent and 'me do it' is a constant demand for everything from dressing to walking the dog.

- They learn to count and reason and recognise their name and other written words.

Parents who may have formerly been comforted that their child is simply a 'slow starter' will no longer be able to accept this for a variety of reasons:

- Mobility aids, splints and callipers, wheelchairs, special seating may become part of the environment.
- Special schooling and the choice of such a school then becomes an issue.
- Exercises are part of the daily routine and often involve coaxing a reluctant child or feeling guilty if other demands crowd out the exercise session.
- Family and neighbours can no longer be deceived. 'He's just a little bit behind' is no longer a valid excuse.

Restrictions and limitations become a part of every disabled child's life. They may have brothers or sisters who do not have such strictures on their lives. Younger brothers and sisters may overtake the disabled child in physical skills. Children become aware that they are different in a negative way. They experience frustration and anger but are often without the means of expressing this. Unexpressed or suppressed anger may result in depression.

A small child with depression will usually benefit from 'games' and non-verbal ways of expressing emotion but a seriously depressed child may not respond to play materials. If the counsellor herself uses the materials, appearing to ignore the child, his interest will often be captured. The counsellor should use the materials in the way she would like the child to, with a quiet commentary on what she is doing. Unless the child offers to join in or asks for a toy the counsellor should not comment to the child or ask for his response. Most children will, if left free to do so, make some move towards a piece of apparatus or toy that attracts them. The toy can be casually moved closer without looking at the child, or he can be asked to hold it in order to facilitate the counsellor's 'game'. Withdrawal should be commented on in a quiet and matter-of-fact way – 'OK, you don't want to hold the doll'. A response should be similarly acknowledged – 'Thank you for holding the doll for me'.

The depressed child needs to feel in control of the situation, as does the fearful child. Depression saps the energy needed to make decisions and any pressure to respond disables the child further. If allowed to take the time that he needs in order to make a decision and to feel safe he will eventually respond, which is in itself great progress.

Teenagers and eating problems

Older children who compare their lives to what they perceive as the lives of other teenagers or who look ahead to their future and prospects may find the perspective depressing. 'Who would ever love me?' is a question expressed by many teenagers. Most parents will have experienced attempting to convince a depressed son or daughter that spots, too much or too little weight, over or under development, spectacles, to give some common examples, will not permanently exclude them from love and relationships. The teenager with a disability will experience all the doubts and mood-swings of adolescence with the additional awareness of a disability.

Pamela was fourteen with mild spastic cerebral palsy. She was very interested in boys and was not attracted to any of the boys in her special needs school – she wanted a 'normal' boyfriend. She defined her problem, explaining 'When I'm sitting down I look normal but as soon as a boy comes up and talks to me I get spasms and make faces and then if I get up he can see how funny I walk.'

Pamela had stopped attending her local youth club and spent much of her time in her bedroom, playing tapes and crying. Her mother became alarmed when Pamela refused breakfast, picked at supper and was reported as 'not eating' at school.

The first approach of the counsellor was to help Pamela recognise that there was a real problem. Pamela denied that she was not eating adequately and insisted that she ate 'when people aren't there'. She was interested in having counselling and agreed to an arrangement whereby she reported to the school nurse every week for a weight check and dietary supervision. She was allowed to bring a packed lunch from home and to choose what she ate from a diet sheet. In return she received a weekly session with the counsellor. With Pamela's consent school staff were consulted and were cooperative.

Pamela's PSE [Personal and Social Education] teacher included in the group curriculum classes in fashion, teenage health problems and beauty care. Keep fit classes were offered by the physiotherapist and the English teacher encouraged the group to produce a teenage magazine which included beauty tips, pop music (and pop groups), a problem page and fashion articles. This project involved the group reading commercial magazines and Pamela reported to the counsellor that 'other kids feel a bit like I do'. Even more surprising to her was to read about able-bodied teenage boys experiencing doubts and depression.

In counselling Pamela was able to explore her feelings about being disabled and to relate her experiences to those of other teenagers, both able and disabled. She became interested in 'how feelings work' and took over the 'problems page' of the class magazine. She ended the counselling after several weeks, saying 'I think my problems are teenage, not disability'. She voluntarily continued her weekly sessions with the school nurse.

Pamela and the counsellor were of course lucky in having the interest and cooperation of the school staff, but most of the activities that helped Pamela could have been undertaken in counselling in some form. Group sessions with other teenagers could also be very appropriate.

Katie, described in Chapter 7, demonstrated depression caused by suppressed anger and guilt and also stopped eating. For some very disabled young people this may be the only way they have of expressing their despair. For those with athetosis, where the maintenance of weight can be a very real problem, this can make adults and professionals, as well as parents, very anxious. The counsellor may well be involved in eating problems.

Often a bargain or 'deal' will help. If a distressed child knows that he will not be nagged about eating, provided that he agrees to have a negotiated minimum of a palatable food he will usually manage to cope with eating. Katie named chocolate gateau as a food she thought she could eat. It was agreed that if she ate one small slice of gateau this would be accepted as adequate, and she also had counselling sessions. The fears of the other adults regarding nutrition were allayed by a recipe being used that included soya flour for protein. Fresh orange slices and vitamin tablets were included to decorate the cream topping and the sliced gateau was kept in the freezer until needed. Once Katie was eating regularly without stress and exploring her feelings in counselling she gradually recovered her appetite.

Some children may accept a nutritionally reinforced drink in a preferred flavour. Others may be able to cope initially with blended food.

It may not seem appropriate for the counsellor to become involved with what is seen as an eating problem (or occasionally even as a disciplinary problem). However, working with the child to identify the possible cause of the difficulty, and exploring with the child an acceptable solution does involve counselling skills. Ongoing support and counselling will often be needed. She may also find herself supporting other staff who feel disturbed or threatened by a child 'refusing' to eat. Adults may be worried that they will be held responsible if the child becomes ill. They may see the refusal as a challenge to their discipline. The child may be described as getting away with unacceptable behaviour, attention seeking or manipulating. All these perceptions will need to be explored and the adults concerned reassured if possible.

Strategies for coping

Taking control can sometimes enable an older child to find a way out of depression.

Penny was an attractive teenager with cerebral palsy, who communicated with Bliss. With a twin sister, Penny experienced a full social life with able peers and was a keen follower of the latest teenage fashions. She and her twin were ingenious in adapting these to meet Penny's needs. Penny always wore one of a selection of bright silk scarves knotted casually around her neck. These matched her clothes – but also absorbed the saliva that Penny could not swallow. The fashionable long skirts covered the callipers and her boots were brightly coloured. Penny always appeared outgoing, bright and cheerful, with a ready smile. However, at times Penny would have bouts of desperate weeping and talked about wishing she were dead. These episodes became more frequent and she requested counselling.

Penny was clearly quite severely depressed. She saw no hope for her future. She wanted a career, a boyfriend and later marriage and children. She felt that she was ugly and conspicuous. She described herself as stupid because she could not speak. She was certain that her parents, her sister and her teachers were all disappointed in her. They were upset, Penny was sure, that she did not try hard enough to master skills with switches so that she could use equipment.

After several sessions Penny was repeatedly referring to other people's opinions of her. The counsellor wondered aloud if Penny was brave enough to check out how people felt about her.

'How?'
'How do you think it could happen?'
'Have a meeting.'
'Who would call the meeting?'
'Me.'
'Who would chair the meeting – lead it, say who was to speak?'
'My sister.'

After discussing all the arrangements that would have to be made, the counsellor said,

'Well, it seems as if you are very well able to organise a meeting. Do you want to?'
'Afraid.'
'What are you afraid of?'
'They say I bad, stupid, ugly.'
'But you have said you believe they think that anyway.'
'Yes.'
'So...?'
'They will be upset.'
'Probably. I would feel upset if I thought my daughter, sister, friend, was feeling as bad about themselves as you are feeling.'
'They feel angry?'
'Maybe with themselves.'
'Why?'
'For not realising how you were feeling and not helping you with your feelings.'
'Angry with me?'

'Absolutely not. Surprised – upset – a bit guilty – concerned – sad – maybe some of those feelings. But for you – not with you. But there is really only one way to find out.'

Penny dictated a letter to arrange the meeting and talked to her sister about what she wanted to say. At the meeting she surprised the counsellor by being calm and controlled, listening intently to everyone as they commented on her impressions of herself. Probably because of Penny's composed manner no-one patronised her by dismissing her concerns and everyone was realistic about the future without ruling out any of Penny's aspirations. Penny was rightly proud of herself and was reassured that her family and teachers understood how hard she was trying and were in fact proud of her progress.

For an adult, to organise good experiences for herself can help relieve depression. Giving oneself a treat is not only reassurance that pleasure still exists but is an affirmation that the person is valuable enough to deserve a treat. It may be listening to favourite music, buying a small treat, using a relaxation tape, having a luxurious bath or massage with essential oils – whatever gives pleasure.

The same strategy can work very well for a child. It can be valuable to discuss with the child what he enjoys and to help him to arrange this. Margaret (see Chapter 12) told the counsellor that when she felt very depressed she watched a tape of her favourite soap from television. 'I go up in my room and close the door. It's a really, really sad episode and I cry and cry about it and then I feel much better!'

It may be necessary to stress that the treat must be possible to organise – a trip to Disneyland® may be appealing but is not very practical. Children like Margaret who devise their own strategies for dealing with depression deserve affirmation and encouragement.

Of course depression may (and probably will) return but if a child has learned that talking about his feelings can help, that it is possible to take action and to hear reassurance and above all that his feelings are acknowledged and not dismissed, then in most cases the depression can be relieved.

Chapter 12

Directed 'Games' and Other Techniques

Non-verbal and sub-verbal ways of enabling children to express and explore their feelings and to begin to find resolutions have already been introduced. In this chapter, some of these techniques are described in detail.

Games provide a safe way for a child to explore possibilities and make statements. He can choose whether or not to accept the counsellor's comments and how much to acknowledge as applicable to himself.

Dolls

Dolls can be of various types:

- Small, flexible 'dolls-house' dolls offer a wide range of possibilities. A set of 'families' of these dolls, black, Asian and white, has twelve dolls in each family. The family includes a grandmother and grandfather, mother and father, teenaged boy and girl, schoolboy and girl, toddler boy and girl and baby boy and girl. Children able to handle these dolls can do so without fear of damage. The dolls can be bent to sit on a table or wheelchair tray and offer a wide range of choice when used to represent family members or other people. They are also very attractive and appealing to children (and adults!) of all ages.
- Plastic play people with movable arms and legs are equally easy and safe to play with although children who have such toys at home or in the classroom tend to identify them with the particular 'set' they are familiar with and refer to them as farmer or fireman, for example.

- Very versatile are simple flexible 'people', easily made with pipe cleaners and small pith balls as heads. These allow identification in any role the child chooses to allocate to them.
- Plastic farmyard and zoo animals are a useful addition to the dolls.

There are many ways to use dolls and animals. A child can be asked to choose dolls or animals to represent himself and any other people he chooses, or if a specific problem is known, the people involved in that problem. Simply asking the child to arrange the dolls (or to direct how they are to be arranged) gives an opportunity for the child to begin to work out feelings and make statements. Part of the counsellor's task is to suggest interpretations of these arrangements.

Shamila, aged eight, was very distressed because her grandmother, who lived with her family, was ill. She chose dolls for each member of her family and arranged them on her tray: father in one corner 'at work in the shop' and mother with him, 'helping father'. Her older brother and sisters were put close together in another corner, 'at school'. Shamila and her grandmother were close together in the centre of the tray. After a moment, Shamila put the grandmother doll's arms around the Shamila doll. The counsellor commented, 'they seem to love each other very much' and Shamila nodded. She then slowly unwound the two dolls and laid the grandmother down. Very slowly, she said, 'the grandmother is very sick.' The counsellor reflected, 'she is very ill.' Shamila hesitated, looked at the counsellor steadily, and then handed the grandmother to her.

'Take her away. She's dead.'
(The counsellor took the doll.)
'Where will you put her?'
'Where would you like her to be?'
'Heaven?'
'You want her to be in heaven? Where is heaven?'
'Up there.'
(Shamila pointed to a shelf where the counsellor displayed flowers and a few pictures.)

With grandmother safe on the shelf, Shamila picked up the child doll.

'She's crying.'
'She's sad.'
'Yes.'

There was a long silence, then Shamila briskly gathered up the dolls and put them away in the box 'all safe together' – except for grandmother. She was left 'in heaven' with the comment, 'She'll be safe there.'

The game described was directed in the sense that the counsellor suggested the characters for Shamila to choose. This gave Shamila permission to then control the play herself and to choose what she disclosed. The counsellor's role was to accept Shamila's script and to affirm her statements.

Shamila had used the dolls to rehearse a situation she feared but in which, with the dolls, she was in control. She had received permission for a death to occur and to feel sad and had affirmed for herself that death was not an end for her grandmother (her family's religion included belief in a happy afterlife). The family was not broken up by the death but was 'all safe together'.

The counsellor may take a more directive role when this is judged appropriate or the child seems unable to play her own script. By asking 'What would happen if...?' or 'I wonder how the boy doll is feeling...?' it is possible to initiate active play.

In other examples of disclosure in a safe activity, a different type of doll can be used. A near toddler-sized rag doll is dressed in baby-sized Piedro boots or Kickers and a unisex track suit. This doll is easily identified as having cerebral palsy or spina bifida, for example, especially if strapped into a baby buggy or small support chair. A symbol chart is also supplied if the child using the doll uses alternative communication.

The child can be introduced to the doll by name, and told that Jane or Jack cannot walk or talk, making the disability mirror that of the child. The child is asked for help. Jane is 'feeling bad' but the counsellor cannot understand what the matter is. Can the child help? Why is Jane feeling bad? What are her feelings?

Louise, always smiling and cooperative, was eight, severely disabled and non-verbal. Introduced to 'Jane' she eagerly indicated the symbols 'angry sad frustrated wheelchair'.

'Jane feels all these difficult feelings because she is disabled? But look at her face – she is smiling.'

'Angry. Sad. Jealous.'

'Right. She has all those feelings – angry, sad, frustrated, jealous. Why is she smiling? Why didn't she tell me?'

'Bad.'

'Who is bad?'

'Doll.'

'So it is bad – naughty – to feel those feelings?'

'Yes'. (emphatically)

'Oh, dear. I will have to explain to Jane that I can understand that she must feel very angry and sad because she can't walk or talk – everyone has those feelings. Poor Jane – of course she is not bad or naughty to have those feelings. She doesn't have to smile all the time.'

Louise looked at the doll and communicated 'want.' When the doll was put on her wheelchair tray Louise looked at her intently for several minutes, making quiet sounds. She then indicated that the counsellor could take Jane back. It seemed clear that Louise had taken the responsibility of explaining to Jane.

A teddy bear with a head that could be moved by manipulating its tail was used by a counsellor to encourage children to answer 'no' as well as 'yes' to questions. Charles would shake his head when asked, 'Are you a happy bear today, Charles?' and in this way give a child permission to talk about his unhappiness if he wished to. Charles developed a personality and became well known. A friend bought him a badge depicting a teddy with the words 'very special person'. When the counsellor saw a pair of miniature glasses on a craft stall she bought them – for Charles. They were safely attached with a length of ribbon. These glasses played an unexpected role in counselling.

Magda was a new child in the school and the counsellor received a message asking her to come to the classroom and to 'bring Charles'. Eight-year-old Magda was full of questions: What did the badge say? Where did he get his badge? The following exchange took place.

'Why has he got glasses?'

'Because he doesn't see so well – like me.' (The counsellor wore glasses.)

'Does he like wearing glasses?'

'Well, yes – he couldn't see properly without them. Anyway, he looks rather clever with his glasses on – and quite handsome, don't you think?'

'Yes. Look – he's saying yes!'

'Yes, he's nodding his head.'

'What's that string for?'

'It's to stop his glasses getting broken. Sometimes they fell off and sometimes he took them off and then he lost them. So the string keeps them safe. Look – I've got a string on my glasses – same reason.'

'Why did he take his glasses off?'

'Well, he wasn't used to them at first and I expect they felt funny. But he's fine now.'

After Magda had examined Charles, his glasses and made him move his head, the teacher thanked the counsellor and she said goodbye. Later, her teacher said that Magda was supposed to wear glasses but was always pulling them off and several pairs had been broken. After meeting Charles, Magda asked for 'a string like Charles' and when supplied with a spectacle retainer wore her glasses quite happily.

Play therapists working in hospitals frequently use dolls bandaged or fitted with appliances similar to those the children have to wear. Play with these dolls and the giving of 'injections' or exercises can help a child come to terms with difficult or painful procedures. The counsellor working with children who have special needs will often find such strategies useful.

Making pictures

Children's drawings can be a valuable indicator of how they are feeling.

When Dylan, aged six, was referred for counselling he came with a history, provided by his teacher, of miserable crying, refusal to walk using his walking frame and frantic clutching of any available adult. He was obviously unhappy but refused to respond to the teacher's approaches.

Dylan seemed happy to be with the counsellor and chose from a number of toys and games. He indicated that he wanted to draw and was offered a box of thick felt pens. He was able to draw despite poor motor control. Choosing a red pen he drew very rapidly and jerkily, every now and then glancing at the counsellor. He carefully fitted the lid back on the pen, then with a green pen scribbled a few additional lines and pushed the paper towards the counsellor.

The counsellor indicated and named parts of the picture and Dylan agreed to eyes, nose, mouth, teeth and hair. He then indicated his own eyelashes and showed them on the picture. Then the counsellor said, 'I wonder if this is a picture of someone special?'

Dylan glanced at her, then nodded. His face crumpled and he pointed at his eyes, miming tears. 'Someone who makes you feel sad?', the counsellor commented. He very rapidly tapped three fingers on his palm, the Makaton sign for mother. He kept his hands half under the table and again glanced at the counsellor.

'So this is a picture of mummy, and you feel sad?'

Dylan did not reply but pushed the box of pens towards the counsellor and put her hand onto the box. 'You would like me to draw a picture. I wonder who I should draw?' asked the counsellor.

Dylan grinned and pointed to the counsellor. He watched as she drew a picture of herself, leaving the face blank. With Dylan's wary agreement she drew a series of pictures representing his teacher and the other adult staff he had contact with. All the faces were left blank. The counsellor then added Dylan and his mother. She then asked how she should draw each face – happy? sad? angry? afraid?

Dylan was very definite: each face in turn was happy. When the picture was finished he clapped his hands and laughed, pointing to each in turn and vocalising an approximation of each name while smiling broadly and tapping each face.

Dylan then took a dark red pen and in contrast to his previous drawing, worked slowly and with great care, looking up and smiling frequently. Yellow, bright red and orange were added with equal care. He stroked the paper very gently and said clearly, 'Sissy!'

The counsellor told him that the session was finished but that he would come back next week. He nodded firmly, handed her his pictures and put her drawing carefully in his bag. He walked with the counsellor back to the classroom.

In subsequent sessions Dylan communicated more about missing his mother and sister and of being afraid that mum saw more of Sissy and loved her more. Each confidence was always preceded by him drawing one of his rapid, jerky pictures, usually in one or, at most, two colours, and finished with a calm and colourful drawing. The counsellor was also enrolled to draw reassuring people and situations.

After ten sessions, Dylan walked happily around school, cried less often and showed an impish sense of humour. He still spoke rarely but communicated effectively with gesture and Makaton.

Making pictures can be as powerful for children who have no hand control.

A group of six- to ten-year-old children, all non-verbal, with athetoid cerebral palsy, was asked to design a collage picture of themselves – but with a difference. The collage was to be in a circle, divided into four segments, each segment representing an element: earth, air, fire and water. This circle form, used in Buddhism as a symbol of the universe, is considered in Jungian psychology as a symbolic representation of the self. The elements arranged in a mandala are a common symbolic representation of the whole self.

It may surprise the reader that children are able to understand such a task. None of the children expressed any surprise and were full of ideas. Each child had an adult helper whose task was to follow the child's design, questioning every stage: colour, position, fabric: every detail. A large selection of fabrics and other materials was available.

John, aged six, chose to divide his circle with curved lines, producing four segments of unequal size. His directions in Blissymbols were:
Earth me come story book.
Air me dad mum brother play.
Fire I secret when angry wheelchair.
Water good down me down fish colours.
With careful questioning John agreed that his pictures were:
Earth – me holding a story book, sitting on sand on a flat beach.

Air – me and dad and mum and my brother playing with a ball in a field.

Fire – this is a secret. When I am angry I imagine my wheelchair is on fire.

Water – it is good to listen to water. A waterfall going down into a little splashy stream, me sliding down the waterfall making a big splash. There are rainbow-coloured fish.

John placed his earth picture in a narrow shape at the top of the circle, fire in the larger corresponding shape below. Two rounded shapes contained water on the left and air on the right. John chose a mixture of fabric collage, drawing and colouring to produce a striking image.

How can what John is communicating be interpreted?

Water represents the emotions, earth the body, air the intellect and fire the sexual, creative energy.

John is highly intelligent, as are his whole family. He recognises this and celebrates his intellect in the joyful game.

His body is not under his control. His physical life is flat and arid. He must use his intelligence (reading a book – a story book) to compensate.

He experiences and plunges into his emotions. Sometimes they sweep him away but into a quiet pool with rainbow fish.

His creative energy, expressing his intelligence and imagination, is frustrated by his disability. He feels furiously angry and his anger wants to destroy the wheelchair, a symbol of his disability, in violent flames. This, he communicated, was a secret, but one he was willing to express in the symbols of a picture.

Sam was ten, severely disabled and non-verbal. Recent deterioration in his abilities had been diagnosed as caused by an inoperable tumour at a high level of his spinal cord. Sam had been told about the tumour but it was generally believed that he had not understood any of what he had been told.

Sam wanted his circle divided into four with two lines crossing. The upper two segments were smaller than the lower two. In the top left segment Sam directed 'Earth fruit orange fire.' In the right segment, 'Fire sun yellow pink orange on purple.' These two images he wanted completed before completing the mandala. The orange on fire was made from orange felt and orange fur fabric on a very dark blue background. The burning sun was a spiked circle of yellow hologram paper with six spikes of deep pink silk radiating from the centre. The background was mauve and blue chiffon.

Sam had been very focused and tense while these images were constructed and wanted others in the group to see them before he continued. The group leader commented, 'So the earth has a burning shape and so does the fire: round shapes of an orange and the sun, with flames? spikes of fire? coming out of them.' Sam beamed and nodded.

He then sighed deeply and instructed, 'Air cloud white sky blue snow ice lake. Water lake flowers birds.' These two calm and beautiful images used sequins for the water-lily centres and some of the snowflakes, the lakes deep blue. Two perky pink and orange ducks of felt and feathers swam on the lily lake. He unexpectedly chose a red silk background for his icy, dark blue and white cotton wool and sequin 'air' picture.

Was Sam saying he knew about the tumour in the burning orange and spiked sun of his 'body' and 'creativity'? Having told us in symbolic form that he did, he then depicted his feelings as a much-loved lake on which he had experienced great happiness in a boat on a school holiday. His intellect was that same lake, frozen and still. Did he want the subject dropped now that we knew? I believe so, and his subsequent relaxed and calm behaviour confirmed this interpretation.

An equally vivid self-portrait was made in a group of older children. Their task was to produce 'a picture that is you' and the counsellor added, 'You can do this in any way you like.'

Richard had been an intelligent, bright and athletic boy until going into a coma after an attack of 'flu' when he was eleven. A degenerative brain disease was diagnosed when he emerged from the coma totally disabled.

Richard was able to indicate 'yes' and 'no' with great difficulty to people who knew him very well and his rapid learning and use of Blissymbols indicated that his intellectual ability was unimpaired. In the years that followed he discussed his disability and death, expressing anger, fear and distress. He gradually became calmer and more positive in his responses. This is described in Chapter 6.

Richard communicated very positively his instructions for his self-portrait. A small white house stood on a dark green lawn. The house had a black door and two pink windows below a dark red roof. A tree on the left with a brown, wool strand trunk and a round top made of overlapping circles of fabric in a number of different shades of green was covered with huge, round flowers with many petals, cut from silver hologram paper. Flowers of lace, net, and flowered fabric bloomed beside the house on the right of the picture. Finally, a bright blue bird of feathers and hologram paper was flying out of the picture on the right.

The house symbol is commonly interpreted as representing the self, the flying bird the soul.
This very positive and beautiful picture of the bird-soul leaving the house-body contrasted with a distressing self-portrait by another member of the group.

Brett was eleven, with emotional and learning disabilities as well as cerebral palsy, and was non-verbal. He was able to walk slowly and could point to symbols and use Makaton signs and gesture to communicate.

Brett came from a very disturbed family background, living mostly with his mother (whom he sometimes mimicked as drinking and staggering) but sometimes with his father and often in respite care. He was a frequent witness of bitter argument between his parents and once communicated that his parents were arguing who should have him. The winner would hand him over to the loser.

Following Brett's directions his self-portrait depicted 'mother angry.' Mother stood with both arms raised and hands clenched in fists. She wore a dark purple trouser suit with a red flower at the waist. She was then outlined with silver glitter-pen and the same pen used to draw a fierce scowl and downturned mouth. Brett looked at this for some time and then giggled. He indicated two pipe cleaners and these were stuck upright beside mother to represent walking sticks.

Brett was very excited by his picture and clasped his hands and cheered, pointing to the sticks and giving the sign for 'mother'. He was revelling in his ability to 'disable' this powerful and angry person.

Using stones

When Richard (see above) was sixteen and in a School Leavers' Group, the teacher/counsellor introduced the eight young people in the group to a collection of stones. These were of all shapes and sizes; seaside pebbles, stones collected in fields, a few polished pebbles, sea-worn glass, fossils, pumice and a piece of rough amber.

Each member of the group was asked to choose a stone for him- or herself. Some knew instantly which stone they wanted; others searched for a long time. Eventually everyone had a stone.

Richard had chosen immediately, a smooth pebble of transparent quartz. Asked to describe it, he gave the symbols, 'strong, beautiful, lonely'. One of the others said, 'strong and beautiful like you, Rich,' and he looked towards her and made the strangled sound that was his strongest affirmative.

When everyone had described their own stone, one, on behalf of the group was asked to arrange the chosen stones in a way he thought represented the group. After deciding that they needed to add the adults, choosing stones to represent them, and much arguing and negotiating, an arrangement that satisfied everyone was decided. The stones were evenly spaced in a circle.

The counsellor then reminded the group that two were leaving school that term. One of these leavers was asked to remove his stone from the circle. The rest decided that the circle would move a little closer in to fill the gap left by his loss.

Richard began to get agitated but agreed to wait until the other leaver had her turn. He was obviously distressed by something.

The leaver removed her stone and the same solution was found in the rearrangement. Someone remarked, 'It's like losing people makes the group feel closer,' and everyone agreed.

Richard by now was very distressed and it was difficult for him to communicate. He eventually gave the symbols 'I go,' and on questioning, it appeared that he wanted his stone removed. When asked, 'Is it you leaving school?' he responded, 'No, dead.'

The counsellor removed Richard's stone and told the group, 'Richard has left the group because he has died.' (His death had been discussed at Richard's request with the group.)

Richard was very tense as the group discussed how to rearrange the stones, someone rejecting every suggestion until the first girl said,

'We'll leave them exactly as they are, the gap is like he is still there, somehow. I know we won't ever forget him but that will be like a reminder.'

Richard relaxed completely and made the slight grimace that was a smile and only appeared when he was totally relaxed. In response to a question he chose to keep his stone until they were all replaced in their bag at the end of the session.

The counsellor knew that Richard's three main fears about his death were that it would be painful, that he would be alone, and that he would be forgotten. The session with the stones did more than anything else to relieve him of the latter, and to him, the most painful fear.

Using the stones to visualise each person and the group they were part of not only clarified the situation for them but enabled feelings to be discussed and clear, caring statements to be made.

The use of stones is a very powerful and versatile technique. It seems that for children and adults, the choice of a stone that is exactly right for them is an act of important and significant meaning. As with the leavers' group, some people will almost grab a stone as soon as they are displayed: others will choose, examine and discard until they find one that is 'right'. In describing the stone, the subconscious reasons for the choice will often become apparent. It would be clear to most counsellors how a client feels about himself when he selects a small, nondescript grey pebble or a dagger-shaped, shiny, black fossil belemnite.

Choosing and arranging stones can enable a child or adult to express feelings about themselves and those around them, to experiment with rearranging their situation or expressing their fears . Having arranged a group of stones to represent his family a child can choose whether to respond to the counsellor's questions and suggestions. 'How would you *like* the family to be arranged? 'What would happen if you took daddy away?' It is safe, the child is in control.

A striking example of a child being very clearly in control and at the same time choosing clearly to make an important statement was a brief exchange with Margaret.

Margaret was a perky, cheerful and outgoing thirteen-year-old with cerebral palsy. Adopted, she had started to talk to the counsellor about her confused feelings regarding her birth mother when she abruptly cancelled a session, saying, 'I'm not allowed to talk to anyone about anything except lessons, so ... I don't really mind,' and went off with a grin and a shrug. Her adoptive parents wrote soon afterwards to ban any counselling or individual work.

In a Personal and Social Education (PSE) class where stones were used, she appeared to seize on the opportunity that her intelligence told her *was* allowed. She was describing a stone, not talking about herself. Margaret chose a pillow-shaped, translucent quartz stone. She said, 'This is an attractive stone, it's smooth and nice to hold. There are no sharp bits, it's really symmetrical. People would think, looking at it, that they could see right through it – but you can't. If you bother to look *really* close there are little marks like writing, below the surface. It's like a language you can't understand.'

The counsellor said, 'May I look?' The response was a casual, 'Of course' accompanied by a very sharp glance. The counsellor examined the stone carefully, handling it with gentleness, and said, 'Yes, I understand what you mean. It is a very special stone with a lot below the surface.'

Nothing more was said at the time, but a year later Margaret told the counsellor that she had informed her parents she needed a private talk, that she had persuaded them to agree, and made an appointment. She started the session with the question, 'Do you remember that stone?'

The counsellor's response was. 'Of course. You told me something that day, I think.'

'Yes,' Margaret agreed. 'I want to talk to you about myself again, now.'

It would appear that her disclosure and its acceptance enabled her to assert herself in stating her needs to her parents and in asking the counsellor to help her meet those needs.

Modelling

Another play activity that can be used constructively is modelling in clay or salt dough. Plasticine is usually too difficult to mould for children with manual disabilities.

Clay, properly prepared and stored, is a very satisfying medium. Some children may be distressed by getting dirty handling clay and if this is a real problem salt dough, made with two cups of plain flour to one of salt, mixed to a firm dough with water, may be preferred.

A child unable to manipulate clay or dough, can direct the modelling in the same way as for collage pictures.

Human figures and all sorts of accessories may be used in the same way as dolls, with the added advantage that the child can destroy a figure, remodel, reshape, or restore it to its original shape. Figures can be kept or stored if that is the child's wish. This can provide a child with a safe way of 'destroying' or otherwise manipulating a hated or feared person – and of expressing angry or destructive feelings without fear.

In the same way that Shamila used dolls to rehearse an anticipated experience, a child can build a world with clay, experiment with a variety of possibilities, test the reaction of the counsellor to his 'game', express feelings and fears: and at the end of the game, put everything safely away.

Role play

Role play can be used either with an individual child or with a group. It can be a useful technique when a child is anticipating a difficult interview.

Tony, eleven, was very worried about a visit to his father, whom he had not seen since Tony had been involved in a car accident that left him with ataxia and partial sight. Tony had received a distraught letter from his father in which extreme statements were made about 'my poor crippled baby boy' and 'it's all my fault not being there, how can I make it up to you.' Tony was an inarticulate, emotional boy and was at a loss at how to respond.

He was unable to imagine what he or his father might say or to express what he most feared. When the counsellor suggested they act a scene about someone in Tony's position he agreed, saying 'I'll be the dad.'

The counsellor played the boy, and the scene developed with the father as an over-the-top tragedy queen and the counsellor taking an anxious, uncertain role as the boy. When the counsellor said, 'Dad, this is really embarrassing me', Tony laughed and said, 'Me too'.

Tony then said, 'You be the father and I'll be the boy.' He efficiently took charge, starting with a calm, 'It's good to see you dad,' and then giving a clear account of the accident and reassurance that he was doing well and enjoying playing football.

His comment was, 'The dad didn't know how to be with the boy, once he knew, he was OK.' The counsellor confirmed that, as dad, she had felt quite relaxed.

Playing the role had given Tony the insight he needed of his father's feelings and the awareness of the need for him to take charge. He reported that the subsequent meeting had gone well 'although dad cried a bit at first.'

In a group, role play can be used to explore a wide variety of interactions from family rows to an appointment at the hospital. Non-verbal children can take part by initially preparing with a helper to speak for them and by then reacting to what is going on, with the helper providing words appropriate to what the child is expressing.

Other techniques

Music

Music can enable a child to contact and identify feelings and make associations. He may wish to discuss these, or may need to just experience a difficult feeling in a safe place. 'Good' feelings may be quietly enjoyed or shared.

A compilation tape can be made, using a selection of short pieces of music in different moods. Using a wide variety of sources including pop, classical, film music, jazz and folk, for example, should enable most emotions to be included. Pieces should be chosen for contrast.

The tape can be used individually or in a group. The child is asked to relax and listen to the first piece of music, and then tell how the music made him feel. He may identify an emotion, such as anger, or make an association, 'It made me think about fighting with my brother.'

The counsellor may invite the child to talk more, or may introduce the next piece of music. A maximum of six contrasting pieces in one session is usually enough.

The counsellor should be prepared for some unexpected reactions. A very lively and humorous piece of barrel organ music reminding most children in a group of parties, dancing, a fair, circus, getting the giggles, but made one little girl contribute, 'afraid – people crying.' She was unable or unwilling to explain and was not receiving individual counselling, but her reaction was definite. It was clearly important to her that she communicate this.

Colours

Colours may be used in the same way as music, to enable children to contact feelings.

Squares of card in a variety of colours are offered to the child one at a time and the child is encouraged to say how that colour makes him feel. He may say as much or as little as he likes. It is important for the counsellor to accept whatever the child says: although as in music, most people share the emotions suggested by a particular colour, individual reactions may vary.

It is very easy to suggest that there is a right or wrong response. In a group, a child told a helper that he thought yellow was an unhappy colour. She responded, 'Oh, I think it's a lovely cheerful colour.' For the rest of the group he listened to what other people were saying before agreeing with the majority. Preparation for the activity should include the information that there are no right or wrong responses: just what the feeling is for the individual.

Colour can also be used to resolve difficult feelings.

Madan, severely disabled with cerebral palsy, non-verbal and with learning disabilities, was very angry. He identified anger as the feeling but was unable to explain why he felt so angry.

He was offered a number of lengths of light fabric (4 to 6 metre lengths of silk or artificial silk are ideal) and asked to choose the one that looked the way he felt. He unhesitatingly chose scarlet, and the counsellor wound the silk loosely around him until he and the wheelchair were completely covered. He looked at himself in a full length mirror and began very deliberately to scream and thrash around under the silk. After a short time he calmed down and began to laugh. The counsellor commented, 'You have been very angry and now you are feeling calmer.' He agreed. Asked if he would like to choose another colour Madan asked for sky blue. Wrapped up as before, he put his head against a fold of silk and closed his eyes. He rested like this until it was time for the session to end. He asked to take the blue silk with him and agreed to return it at the end of the day. He left the counselling room calm and smiling.

Relaxation

Relaxation, taught and practised either individually or in a group, can greatly reduce stress and depression. In athetoid cerebral palsy the ability to consciously relax can not only help control excessive movement but is also a valuable way of managing emotional overflow and lability. Spastic muscles can relax. Pain relief can result. For almost every type of disability and illness, deep relaxation and visualisation provide a happy experience that can be recalled and used when the child is unhappy, sleepless, disturbed or afraid.

The technique

The technique needs to be adapted from that commonly used. This is most important for children with muscle spasm or uncoordinated movements but is helpful for all children.

The child must be in a relaxed and supported position. For some, a beanbag, with extra pillows for support where necessary, is most comfortable. Others may be more comfortable lying on a foam mattress, with or without pillows. Small children are often most comfortable and relaxed resting between an adult's legs, the adult sitting on a beanbag. In this position very gentle restraint can help control excessive movement and spasm. Older children, particularly if being moved is painful, may prefer to rest in their chairs with their head resting on a pile of pillows. Boots and callipers should be removed and any tight clothing loosened. A light blanket may be appreciated.

The room should be warm but not hot and the lighting subdued. A shaded light on the floor is better than overhead lights. The room should be free from any interruption or sudden noise. A few drops of lavender or bergamot essential oil in a small bowl of water over a burner or on a radiator aids relaxation.

Tapes can provide a soft, regular background to relaxation and minimise startle reflex, or excitement by sudden noise or movement. Quiet music is appropriate but anything with a tune should be avoided.

Natural sounds such as waves breaking on a shore, rain falling or running water are helpful.

The voice should be quiet, slow and almost monotonous in tone. Use of words with sibilance and repetition of words and phrases are all aids to deep relaxation.

Images that are useful are those which suggest safety, warmth and comfort. It is not helpful to ask the child to control his breathing in any way because in many cases this is impossible and any effort is destructive. He can usefully be asked to visualise the warm air flowing into and filling his body. For reasons which should be clear, any exercises involving tightening and then relaxing muscle groups are not appropriate. Images such as 'floppy as an old sock' and 'float like a piece of seaweed' are more likely to help muscle relaxation.

Counting slowly to ten can help deepen the state of relaxation but should be accompanied by word pictures such as 'One – you are floppy, floppy. Two – your arms are floating in the warm sea' and so on. In the script which follows the numbers are disguised in the script but are just as powerful, if not more so.

About twenty minutes to half an hour should be allowed for a deep relaxation session, with the child allowed to rest quietly after the exercise. Some children may fall asleep. When ending the session this should be done quietly and gradually, the child being encouraged to 'wake up', stretch, yawn and begin to move while the lights are slowly brightened and movement increases.

As a conclusion and reinforcement afterwards, children often enjoy talking about what they visualised and this can help maintain the good feelings.

Relaxation script – sea images

Rest comfortably, feeling your whole body growing soft and floppy. Soft and floppy. Soft. Rest quietly and let soft, rainbow bubbles float softly through your head and body. Soft, rainbow bubbles quietly floating through your whole body and head.

None of the sounds in the room will disturb you while you rest softly on the pillows. Nothing will make you jump or startle you in any way. Any sounds will simply make more soft bubbles to float through your arms – softly float through your legs – your head – your tummy –

rainbow bubbles softly floating through your back and neck. Let your eyes softly close and the bubbles float softly through your eyes.

It is good, very good, to feel warm and safe, softly supported on the pillows, held safely and softly like a sleepy baby in his mummy's arms, soft and safe.

Sometimes hearing counting softly from one to ten can help you feel softer and floppier, help you float with the bubbles.

As you listen to the soft swish of the waves on the sandy shore, warm waves swishing on the shore, feel the warm, soft sand underneath you, holding you safely. *One* of the lovely things about the seaside is the gentle sound of the waves, swishing up the beach and softly sloshing down, no *two* waves the same, soft and soothing.

With the sound of the sea and the soft sand holding you, feel the warm sun on your body, warm sun, warm sand. A cool breeze slides across your face, across your skin. Sounds and feelings, soft and safe and warm.

Use a *third* sense and taste the salty sea on your lips, taste the cool breeze and the salty taste of the sea. Listen and feel and taste *for* all these things are safe and soft and warm.

See the deep blue of the sky with small, fluffy white clouds softly moving across the blue sky. See the blues and greens of the sea with silver foam as the waves rise and fall. All *five* senses helping you feel soft and safe and warm. As you rise and fall with the waves let your body softly *sink* into the warm sea, the sea which will hold you safe in its arms, soft and warm. Let the waves lift and lower you and the *seventh* wave raise you higher as it sways you up and down like a piece of seaweed, soft and floppy, before the *eighth* wave takes you in its arms.

Rest in the deep, warm sea, be*nign* mother of all life, soft and safe, holding you *ten*derly in its arms.

The sea is the mother of all life, from the tiny, brightly coloured creatures that sway in the blue and green and silver waves, the shining, beautiful fish that flash through the deep blue water to the great, calm, gentle whales that move in the purple deeps. Everything is precious in the sea, from the tiny, softly coloured creatures to the great whales that sing in the deeps, everything is precious and nothing is wasted. When the creatures of the sea die, their bodies sink softly into the warm deeps and become part of the great, beautiful sea and make new lives to move softly in the warm sea. Every tiny creature, every fish, every seal and whale and dolphin, every frond of seaweed and small shellfish is precious. Everything is precious, nothing is wasted, every life is special.

Float your arms out softly in the warm sea and feel the fish sliding past you, their soft cool bodies, sliding past you. See the shining, smiling dolphins as their warm bodies slide past and their wise eyes smile at you. Play with the dolphins, twisting and turning in the warm water, safe and warm. Feel all the feelings of anger and guilt and fear, all the difficult feelings melting into the warm water. Softly sliding away from you into the accepting sea, melting away and made precious in the sea, swirled away by the sea and the dolphins, leaving you soft and warm and safe.

Soon it will be time to leave the sea for a time. It will always be there, there with the dolphins and the fish, the seaweed and the creatures, warm and safe and beautiful, special and precious to you.

Whenever you want to go back to the sea, to feel warm and safe and soft, special and precious, all fear and pain dissolved away into the soft water, all you need do is say the word 'soft' to yourself. Soft. See the word 'soft' in the beautiful colours of the sea, blue and green and purple and silver. Hear the word 'soft' with the swish and slosh of the waves. Soft. Soft. Soft. Your own special dream, your own special sea dream. Soft and warm, soft and safe. Soft. Your own magic word. Soft.

In a few moments I am going to count to five and you are going to come softly back from the sea, back to the warm room, back to the soft pillows.

One – you are beginning to come back from the sea . . .
Two – you are beginning to feel the pillow you are resting on . . .
Three – you begin to hear small sounds in the room, feel your body on the beanbag or mat . . .
Four – feel your body beginning to stretch and wriggle . . . open your eyes . . .
Five – wake up – look around you – come back into the room . . . don't forget your magic word . . . wide awake now!

Children do not seem to have any difficulty in expressing themselves symbolically and in understanding symbolic play. Their everyday world is full of associations and meanings that in most adult's experiences are forgotten or suppressed. Symbolic associations that may appear in an adult's dreams or are subconsciously expressed in adult's paintings or poetry are easily understood by a child. Children will readily use this form of expression to communicate deep feelings and beliefs.

Chapter 13
The Counsellor and Client

Who is the counsellor?

It is assumed that whoever undertakes the counselling of children who are disabled or ill has counselling qualifications, a diploma or certificate from a recognised counsellor training course. However, awareness of the problems that may be experienced by such children and of the techniques that can enable them to express difficult feelings can only enhance the skills of anyone working with distressed children and benefit the child.

Sadly, there are very few qualified and experienced counsellors outside specialist centres working with children who are disabled. A teacher, therapist, social worker, support staff member – all may find themselves approached by a child needing emotional support.

Of course, when a child is obviously seriously disturbed, counselling is not an adequate response. A clinical psychiatrist will be the appropriate referral. The local health authority may have special clinics, the school may have access to a clinical psychiatrist or a child guidance clinic may be available. Sadly, in many areas such help is not available or long waiting lists exist. Counselling may be the only option.

However, for very many children who ask for help counselling will be appropriate.

Most trained counsellors have the core skills necessary for counselling children. Some of the special skills that need to be developed are suggested in this book. The special area of disability and illness does require some extra knowledge and skills which can be acquired by working with other professionals with the relative experience and relating their knowledge to the demands of a counselling relationship.

Professionals with experience of children who are disabled or ill can develop the counselling skills necessary to help these children with their emotional difficulties. A recognised counselling course will offer little in this specialist field. Courses in counselling skills are designed for the student to learn basic counselling skills and to practise these with clients. A course may refer to some particular client groups but unless there is a student on the course with a particular interest in, and knowledge of, disability this may not even be mentioned.

The contract

Every counselling relationship must depend on a contract between the counsellor and the client. The contract consists of an agreement, verbal (although it may be advisable to record this) or written, concerning confidentiality, the time and number of sessions, the boundaries of the relationship and the expectations of both parties.

Confidentiality

This is one of the most fundamental aspects of the counselling contract and must be very carefully considered before any counselling is undertaken. A client asking for counselling often feels that what he has to disclose is intensely personal and private and relies on the professional ethics of the counsellor that what he says will remain strictly confidential. Every counsellor needs to be very clear where the boundaries of confidentiality are drawn for her and to make these clear when establishing the initial contract.

A child will frequently insist that what he has to say is a secret and will demand a promise from the counsellor that she will tell nobody. This is clearly not acceptable for a number of reasons. The counsellor may have professional constraints and may be answerable to a superior for any information she has about a child. Equally importantly her responsibility for the welfare of a child should prevent her from remaining silent if the child tells of abuse. The vital point is that whatever constraints the counsellor has are clearly conveyed to the child before counselling starts.

This can be stated quite clearly and simply:

'What we talk about will be private to you and me. I will not talk about anything you tell me. But there are two things I must tell you. I have to let Jane know if you tell me anything that might make a difference to your treatment. Suppose you told me that you didn't take your medication? I would do my best to help you sort out what the problem is but Jane would have to know, you might get very ill and she would have to know why.

The other thing is also to stop you being badly hurt or made ill – that is, if anyone is hurting you or being cruel to you in any way. I would have to tell someone who could stop that happening. I would feel the same if you told me that was happening to another child. I will never tell anyone without letting you know, and you will have the chance of being there if you want to.'

In many years' experience, sometimes involving abuse, no child has ever refused counselling on these terms. Often a child gives the impression that for someone else to take on the responsibility of dealing with what is happening is an enormous relief.

The time and duration of sessions

This needs to be established. A counselling session is usually 50 minutes. For some children, especially those with a short attention span or a physical condition resulting in fatigue, a shorter session may be more appropriate. The demands of a school timetable or treatment may have to be considered. Whatever time is decided, it is very important that the time is adhered to. There is safety for the child who can then be secure in knowing that he can be in control of how much he discloses within a set time.

Of course, some children may demand extra time, introduce a very important topic just at the end of the session or become very distressed during the last few minutes. Most counsellors will recognise this behaviour as common to many adult clients. As with adult clients, acknowledging the topic introduced with the promise to talk about it at the next session is the appropriate response. The counsellor will need to time the session to avoid leaving the client, child or adult, too upset to finish at the correct time.

Some children will need only one session to resolve a problem. For some, the initial session seems to satisfy the immediate need and the child clearly wants time before another session. Others may need several sessions to work through whatever is distressing them. In the latter case it is advisable to set a number of sessions at the start, offering four or six. This can be extended if at the end of the course there is a need for further work.

A session once a week would be the average arrangement and most children are able to accept and plan for this. The possibility of increasing the number of sessions, or altering the length of sessions originally planned for less than the standard fifty minutes, may be offered if the counsellor's timetable permits and she feels that it is appropriate.

The boundaries

The boundaries of the relationship need to be clearly defined to avoid fantasies about the counsellor's involvement with the child. The contract regarding time will help to establish this but it is also important that the child understands that counselling is a job, like teaching or therapy. This does not mean that the counsellor does not care very much about the child and wants to help – but the counsellor is not a special friend outside the counselling relationship. The aim of the counselling is to help the child find solutions for difficulties or the resolution of intractable problems. Solutions may be possible when, for example, the problem involves relationships or attitudes. Such problems can often be solved. Problems that may be intractable are, for example, the child's inability to walk or speak or their impending death. In these circumstances counselling aims to help the child express painful feelings, to find a way of coming to terms with them and to recognise and value gifts and abilities. The counsellor can offer additional help and support where this is appropriate.

The expectations

The expectations of the child need to be understood and the counsellor must be clear about what she can offer. Children usually understand if they are told that the counsellor does not have a magic wand, much as she may wish she had. In some situations the counsellor may be able only to listen, accept and validate the child's feelings. She cannot reverse brain damage or halt the progress of disease.

Ending counselling can be difficult and the child needs to be clear that counselling is for a limited period only. Ending counselling is discussed in Chapter 15.

Supervision

Supervision for the counsellor is essential. Supervision in this sense will be regular sessions with another counsellor, preferably but not essentially someone working in the same broad area, or with a colleague who has counselling skills. Supervision has the following benefits:

- It provides a number of vital supports to the counsellor.
- It allows for evaluation of the counselling work which is important for the learning and development of the counsellor, as well as ensuring that the child is receiving the best help the counsellor can give.
- It provides an opportunity to discuss possible approaches with a particular child and gives the counsellor perspective on the counselling process.
- Emotional release and support for the counsellor in a safe environment with a skilled supervisor is important. Counselling children with severe disabilities or terminal illness is very distressing and the resolution of painful emotions is as important for the counsellor as it is for the child.
- The identification and resolution of any personal problems that may be blocking the counsellor's ability to work with a particular child will not only enable the counsellor to continue productive work but also contribute to her own growth.

Parental involvement

Whether or not parents are involved in their child's counselling is a difficult issue. Sometimes there is no discussion. The rules of the school, hospital or residential home may require the parent's permission for their child to receive counselling. This refers to formal counselling, but leaves the counsellor who works in the establishment with the problem of protocol and humanity when approached informally by a very distressed child. Then it is worth requesting a discussion with the management for a reconsideration of the rule, stressing the professional standards of counselling and offering examples of the counselling contract. If this is rejected then the child must be informed that his parents must be involved if he wants more than an informal chat.

In other work situations it is not considered necessary to inform parents, especially if the counsellor is one of the staff. The counsellor can then decide when it will be constructive to involve the parents (as is often the case) and when the child's problems would be increased by doing this. Of course the automatic notification of parents would need to be made clear when contracting for confidentiality. The child's permission must be obtained if this has not already been established.

Other disciplines

In some circumstances the counsellor may feel strongly that other agencies involved with the child need to be informed about issues raised in counselling. Again, she can suggest to the child that this would be helpful and ask his permission to approach a particular person. It must be made clear to anyone contacted in this way that the information is confidential. It is a sad fact that many professionals find it difficult or impossible to accept that children have any right to confidentiality or privacy and this is especially true when that child is disabled.

The headteacher of a school for children with special needs initially expected the counsellor to give him a written report detailing what a child said in each counselling session. After discussion he reluctantly agreed that this was not appropriate. A physiotherapist demanded that the counsellor tell her if a child had been complaining about his parents as she 'knew the family and they were very caring parents'. The therapist was very angry when the counsellor declined to discuss the session. A child remarked to the counsellor that 'in this place everybody from the Head to the bus driver knows all your business, if you have a pee it's in the school newspaper next day.'

Personal skills

It has been said that if you have an overwhelming wish to help and care for children you should not work with them. The truth behind that rather cynical saying is that such a person is more likely to want to take over and dictate 'what is best' for a child and to protect them from a reality that might be painful.

Important attributes that a counsellor should have are: a respect for the strength of children, the ability to believe that a child can make choices about his life, accepting that a child must be allowed sometimes to make the 'wrong' choices and supporting him in his choice, realising that oneself can be wrong and admitting it to the child, accepting that some circumstances are intractable, and a realisation that children can teach a great deal.

It will also be important to be flexible, preparation for a session must also allow for the possibility of the child deciding what his own needs are.

The ability to focus completely on the child is essential especially when there are communication problems.

There are some personal skills that the counsellor will need to develop to enable her to counsel effectively children who are disabled or ill. A personal development programme will provide a check list:

- **Self awareness.** I need to recognise and come to terms with my own less-acceptable feelings about disability and my own fears of illness. I need to be aware of my resentment about demands made on me. I must recognise fears I may experience about my motives for working with disability and accept that these are natural. I must watch for my hidden agendas for the children I work with.

- **Readiness to learn.** I need to learn from the children, their parents and other disciplines. I need to attend courses, read, and listen to other counsellors.

- **Flexibility.** I need to keep an open and questioning mind and never make agendas, stereotype or make assumptions about children. I must never think of myself as *the* expert.

- **Ability to change.** I need to accept that I will sometimes change my ideas, my approach, and my opinions – however painful and difficult this is.

- **Acceptance of failure.** I am not the right person for everyone and I do not possess a magic wand. It is alright to fail sometimes. I must be prepared to take risks.

- **Willingness to teach.** If my skills are effective they can be passed on. The purpose of my experience is the sharing of it with others for the benefit of the children. Egocentricity and exclusivity are not helpful.

- **Care for myself.** I must arrange supervision and ask for care and support when I need it. I must never feel I can 'go it alone' both for myself and for my effectiveness as a counsellor.

- **Acceptance of the 'goodies'.** Counselling involves the trust and confidence of the child, seeing that child with my help resolve problems and cope with difficult emotions. It feels good to be a counsellor in these situations. There is not only nothing wrong with feeling good, it is essential. It is the only acceptable reason for doing the work.

Chapter 14
The Skills

The reader will probably be from any one of a variety of backgrounds and skills. It may be that a professional training in one of the medical or paramedical professions has given knowledge of disability and disease. A teacher training will include awareness of child development: further training in special needs will add another dimension of knowledge. Direct experience of working with or bringing up a disabled child is another field of knowledge. A trained counsellor will have specialised knowledge of emotional difficulties.

In this chapter it will be assumed that the reader has experience in some, but not all, of these areas.

What do you need to know?

Medical information

In Chapter 2 some of the common disabilities and possible associated emotional difficulties are described. It is important that the counsellor be informed about the causes and effects of the disability or illness affecting the child. General information is often available, in leaflet form, from the many organisations relating to specific disabilities. Some examples are SCOPE (cerebral palsy) and ASBAH (spina bifida and hydrocephalus). Details of these and other organisations and groups not included in the Useful Organisations list can be obtained from the *Directory for the Disabled* and *A Practical Guide for Disabled People* (see Reading List).

Information about a particular child may be more difficult to elicit due to various concerns including confidentiality. In a school, the school nurse or doctor or the child's teacher may be helpful, especially when the professional commitment to confidentiality of the counsellor is understood. (See Chapter 13 and the check list later in this chapter.) In a hospital, access to the child's notes may be possible.

It is clearly essential that the counsellor understands the physical difficulties a child is experiencing, the possibility of a terminal condition and the likely progress of an illness before she can assess the emotional content of what she is told. In addition it has been stressed in Chapter 5 that the child needs clear and accurate information about his disability and it is often the role of the counsellor to give this information, or at the very least to help the child find out what he needs to know.

Social factors

Clearly it will be helpful, especially when working with younger children, to know if, for example, the child is living at home or in care; if both parents are involved in his life; if there are religious or cultural aspects of his life. The older child may well wish to decide what information he gives the counsellor. Where there are communication problems this may be difficult for him and he may be happy to give permission for the counsellor to ask about his background. I am not suggesting a full social report, simply facts that are relevant to the situation.

Communication problems

Chapter 3 describes ways of working with a child who has speech or language problems or who uses alternative or augmentative communication. It will be helpful for the counsellor to initially observe the child talking to his teacher, therapist or parent and to join in a general conversation. It is important to be honest with the child if the therapist is unfamiliar with the communication system, to be relaxed and to accept the possibility of misunderstanding. It cannot be repeated too often that anyone with speech difficulties would prefer to repeat himself until he is understood rather than know the other person is pretending to understand or is assuming she knows what he wants to say.

Reflect back on what you have understood, 'Have I got this right? You are telling me that you feel frustrated?' If you are really unsure, say so, 'I may have got this wrong, if so I apologise, but I think you are saying that you are frustrated.'

If you cannot understand, ask if you may question and use 'arrow' questions: 'Is it a feeling you are describing? Is it a good feeling? Is it a difficult feeling? I will say (or show you pictures of) some feelings. Tell me when I say the right one.'

Counselling skills

The specific skills described here, empathy, congruence and non-possessive warmth, are those of client-centred, non-directive counselling. These skills may need adaptation to work with children and some adaptations are discussed.

Empathy

> *The counsellor, without prejudgements or assumptions, allows herself to be open to perceive the world as the client sees it. She conveys this understanding to the client, mainly by reflection.*

Empathy can be difficult when working with children. Adults are accustomed to teaching and directing children. A responsible adult will point out when a child has misunderstood or misjudged a situation. She will use her knowledge and experience to advise or direct the child.

The role of the counsellor is different, and the teacher or parent must be aware of the need to consciously change her role. She must initially empathise with the child and enter his world. Her response to 'Everybody hates me' is not, 'I'm sure you have lots of friends' or 'Perhaps you need to be kinder to other children' but 'You feel that everybody hates you. That sounds like a very unhappy feeling.'

When the child feels that he is understood and accepted he will be able to explore, and begin to resolve, previously unexpressed feelings that he may feel are shameful, stupid or wicked.

Congruence

> *The counsellor recognises her own feelings and shares these with the client, when this is appropriate.*

Children in particular may be very aware of the counsellor's reactions to what they are saying and may well misinterpret those feelings. A counsellor may feel very angry if she is told of abuse or neglect. The child may well interpret what he observes as anger directed at himself. To be congruent, to say to the child 'I am feeling very angry that these things were done to you' both affirms and reassures him.

Fourteen-year-old Winston came to the counsellor after a doctor's appointment. His usual cheerful and confiding manner was absent, he looked sad and depressed. It took some time before he told the counsellor that the doctor was pleased with the extensive plastic surgery carried out on his face and he needed no more operations. That was good, he said, he was glad he now had a 'good face.' 'People don't stare at my face no more.' He then hesitated, and holding up his deformed hands, burst into tears. The counsellor discovered that the doctor had taken Winston's hands, turned them over and said, 'Let's have a go at these ugly old things next, shall we?' Winston sobbed, 'I didn't know my hands was ugly, I is so, so ugly.'

The counsellor was overcome with sadness and anger at what had happened and at Winston's grief and bewilderment. She was unable to speak and Winston looked up. He stared at her, and spoke softly and wonderingly. 'You is *crying*! You has tears! Is you crying for *me*?' The counsellor answered that she felt very angry that the doctor had been so unkind and that Winston felt so unhappy. Yes, his hands looked different but they were clever hands and kind hands and therefore couldn't be ugly. Winston grinned. 'These hands going to make us a cup of tea, yes? Then they be beautiful, eh?'

Winston decided that he did not want surgery on his hands. He could do anything he wanted to with them and frequently offered to help 'with my beautiful hands.' His only further comment was 'That doctor very clever with face, not so clever with people.'

Of course there will be times when it would be quite inappropriate for the counsellor to share her feelings with the child. It is important that she recognises and acknowledges to herself what she is feeling. She must ensure that her voice and manner do not suggest to the child that he is responsible for any adverse reaction.

Non-possessive warmth

The counsellor communicates a concern for the whole person of the client, a concern that is not influenced by any preconceived ideas nor by any plans or decisions the counsellor may have been tempted to make for the client.

This is perhaps the most difficult skill of all to practice when working with children who have special needs. Such children frequently have limited opportunities for making and carrying out decisions and may want or need help. It is easy for the counsellor to feel that she is the only person who knows the child's real needs and to become possessive of that child. There will be times when the assumption may be true but the possessiveness is still not appropriate. To write the script for the child, to decide on what is the best course of action, is to deny the child his right to make his own decision. To deny him possible access to other sources of help and support is to make him dependent and again denies his fundamental right of choice.

Words frequently heard from professionals are 'my class', 'my child', 'my patient', 'my client' and such possessive phrases need careful consideration. They are most frequently heard when any decisions about the child are being discussed and may betray agendas that relate more to the adult's need to be the most significant person in the child's life, to be the one with special understanding, than to the child's needs. 'He and I have a special relationship' is a phrase that reflects more of the adult's need to feel special than the child's perception of the relationship.

The counsellor may sometimes find herself in the position of conveying the child's needs to others. As well as monitoring her own feelings towards the child the counsellor will need to be aware of the possible threat she may be to other adults who need to feel special for that child, his parents being an obvious example. The counsellor should act as go-between for the child and be very clear when she is passing on the child's wishes and when she is expressing her own opinions.

A check list

When the counsellor has the relevant information about the child and is familiar with counselling skills, the following check list summarises points that will need to be considered when working with a child who has special needs.

- **Confidentiality**. Decide under what circumstances, and to whom, you would feel it necessary to pass on anything the child might tell you. Make this clear to the child before starting to listen to confidential disclosures. If you decide that you are going to pass on information under this agreement, inform the child. Offer him the opportunity of being present whenever possible.

  Make sure that the counselling session takes place somewhere the child feels safe from being overheard. If this is not possible at the time you are approached, offer a time when you can meet in a confidential setting. Make this as soon as possible. Children will usually be well able to cope with a delay.

- **Respect the child**. Establish an atmosphere of trust and respect. Trust what the child says and respect his feelings.

  If you do not feel able to cope with the situation, offer the child the opportunity of talking to someone you feel could help. Remember, though, that if a child chooses to talk to you that often means that you are the right person for that child.

- **Enabling**. Use permission-giving techniques – games and activities that teach the child that he does not have to conform to any preconceived ideas or expectations. In these games there are no right or wrong answers, no winners or losers.

  If you need to confirm information the child is giving or need to convey that you think the child is fantasising, do so without condemnation or criticism. Own your doubts. Not, 'That can't be true' but 'I can't work out how that could have happened. Can you help me? Is that how you thought it might have happened?'

- **Asking questions**. If you need to ask questions to clarify a confusion or to expand inadequate messages, own your confusion and say that you need to ask questions. Acknowledge that you may ask some silly questions and will need to be corrected. Ask several questions, the least likely first, to avoid 'leading' or jumping to conclusions.

- **Observation**. Observe body language. A child may say he is 'fine' but avoid eye contact. He may fidget more than usual. Gripping the chair, 'fiddling' with toys or clothing, glancing round, may all indicate tension. Be aware that a child with athetosis will 'fidget'. Tension may be due to spasticity.

If you are clear that the body language is expressing contrary feelings, refer to this. 'Can you look at me and tell me how you are feeling?' 'Your hands don't seem to be very happy.'

Be aware of the possibility of stereotyping. Many children with hydrocephalus have a poor grasp of reality and fantasise or exaggerate – but not all. Many children with head injury are abnormally sensitive to real or imagined slights – but some are abused. There are many other examples. Challenge obvious impossibilities or contradictions but acknowledge and respect the child's pain, which is real.

- **Allow feelings.** Recognise and acknowledge any anger, grief, fear, jealousy or resentment expressed by the child. Give permission to experience difficult feelings. Avoid the term 'bad feelings' which for many children is interpreted as 'wrong, wicked feelings'. Saying, 'That would make me feel very angry, I think', or 'I would feel jealous of someone who could do all those things when I couldn't' for example, are much more enabling.

  Owning such feelings yourself demonstrates that they are acceptable. Stating that they are natural in the circumstances helps the child own their difficult emotions.

  Do not say 'I know how you feel' or 'I know what it's like.' Everyone's experiences are different. It is helpful to share feelings, particular emotions in words such as 'I don't know what it is like to have that happen to me but I do know what it is like to feel very jealous.'

- **Offer strategies.** Help the child find ways of resolving difficult situations and feelings. Suggest 'What would happen if . . .' or 'How would it be if . . .'

  It may be useful to offer to facilitate meetings between the child and another person or people. Charlie (see Chapter 8), with his mother, and Penny (see Chapter 11),with her family and school staff, both found meetings helpful.

- **Look after yourself.** Counselling children can be a stressful and sometimes a distressing experience. Contract for supervision with a colleague with counselling skills, another counsellor or counsellor supervisor. Confidentiality is of course essential in supervision.

  Use supervision to evaluate and monitor your counselling, to identify and resolve your own difficult feelings related to the counselling and to discuss its future development.

- **Be realistic.** Some of the problems experienced by children with disability or illness are intractable. No counsellor can heal the brain damage causing cerebral palsy nor prevent the progress of muscular dystrophy. Be clear about what it is possible to achieve and make sure that the child knows that you do not possess a magic wand.

  That stated, do not underestimate the value of responding to a child's emotional needs with respect and empathy. Many children can be enabled to identify, acknowledge and resolve some of their pain and bewilderment and to develop emotional wholeness.

Chapter 15
Moving On and Growing Away

Ending counselling

The issue of timing and duration of counselling was discussed in Chapter 13 and it was suggested that an initial number of sessions be decided on at the start of counselling. A course of four to six sessions was suggested.

It may be that such a course of counselling will be sufficient to resolve whatever situation has brought the child to the counsellor. Some problems can be identified, the feelings expressed and a satisfactory resolution reached. The child himself will often suggest that he does not need counselling help any more or will be happy when the original contract ends. Pamela (see Chapter 11) ended the counselling herself when she felt comfortable in doing so.

Continuing counselling

In other cases the counsellor may feel that more time is needed. In these circumstances it is appropriate to extend the number of sessions, again with a definite number suggested and mutually agreed.

What is not recommended is an open-ended arrangement with an indefinite number of sessions. There is a very real risk that the child will become deflected from the work related to his deep feelings and use the sessions to talk about everyday problems. He can then avoid resolving these problems himself, avoid taking responsibility for them, and the counselling sessions settle into a rehearsal of minor grievances and complaints.

A child can become dependent on the counsellor and search for problems to present. The undivided attention and affirmation of an approving adult is a very desirable thing and some children crave such attention. This is an undoubted need but not one that is appropriate for the counsellor to provide on a long-term basis.

Long-term counselling

Some children, with serious difficulties caused by intractable problems, may well need more than one series of counselling sessions. The counsellor may find that she is providing a sequence of crisis interventions without the basic issues ever being resolved. This may be the best that is possible for the child. The alternative, that of long-term, in-depth counselling, needs very careful consideration. The counsellor must discuss with her supervisor what would be the goals of such an arrangement. A clear plan must be decided. I am not suggesting that agendas or expectations are defined but the long-term aims need definition. This must also be discussed with the child and made clear to him that work and commitment will be expected.

Both Richard (Chapters 6 and 12) and Denny (Chapter 8) in each case had long-term counselling, in both cases with considerable success. In both cases, with their consent, some of the tasks involved were discussed with others. Richard had support from his teacher and the speech and language therapist and Denny included his mother in many of his sessions. This enabled both of them to practise new skills and understandings with people who would understand and support what they were doing.

This additional support must be structured and discussed openly with everyone concerned. It must be clear that the counselling sessions are the focus. The understanding must be that only one person – the counsellor – is the recipient of confidences related to the task. This will avoid confusion and possible manipulation by the child or other adults involved. No client can work effectively with more than one counsellor and the client/counsellor relationship should be on that professional understanding.

Whether the counselling relationship is short or long term, one overriding aim must be that of the child developing and practising choice and responsibility in managing his problems. It must be understood that the counsellor's role is not to make decisions for the child. It is also important that the child is encouraged to use the counsellor's skills to clarify his feelings and actions and to develop his own strategies for helping himself.

If the counsellor's situation permits it can be helpful to offer the opportunity for one or two sessions at some prearranged future time. This is to evaluate how the child is managing. It also reassures the child that the counsellor is genuinely interested and could be available if his situation needs further input.

Growing away

There will be a time when the opportunity of working with the counsellor is no longer available. The child will need preparation in building his own network for support. His needs will mainly be dictated by his individual situation. Counselling support may not be necessary at the time of withdrawal but may be needed again at some time in the future. It may not then be readily available.

In school or college

If the child remains in school or college for a number of years after counselling ceases it will be helpful to discuss with him what help will be available within that structure. Children may need help in identifying the appropriate person for particular needs. Discussing with the child who he would like to talk to in specific situations will clarify his expectations and the areas where information is needed.

Some children find concrete examples easier to understand. A 'help sheet' could be filled in after discussion and will provide the child with a record of his idea (see Fig. 15.1).

Leaving school

If the child is moving away from the area then a similar exercise will help him anticipate what help may be available in his new school and neighbourhood.

When a young person is leaving school it may be to attend college or to move into a residential setting. The counsellor could be involved in helping him find out about what will be available should he need

Who could you talk to about a problem you might have? Tick the people you might ask.

Mum   Gran (Nan)   Aunt   Sister

Dad   Granpa (Pop)   Uncle   Brother

Anyone else in the family (name) . . . .

Adult friends (names) . . . .

Child friends (names) . . . .

Headteacher
Deputy Head
Department Head
Class teacher
Other teachers (names) . . . .
Class assistants (names) . . . .
School doctor . . . .   Speech therapist . . . .
School nurse . . . .   Physiotherapist . . . .

Social worker
Anyone else (names) . . . .

You can use this chart to decide who you could go to if:

> You are being bullied or teased in school
> You are being bullied or teased outside school
> Someone is hurting you
> Someone is making you do something you don't want to do
> You are being abused
> You are worried about a friend
> You are worried about your brother/sister
> You are worried about your parents
> You have questions about your disability
> You have questions about your future
> You have difficult feelings
> You are afraid of someone
> You have problems with sex or relationships
> Any other problems

Fig. 15.1 Help sheet example.

counselling or emotional support and information. He could be helped, for example, to compose a letter asking if there is a college counselling service or a drop-in centre for disabled young people.

A prepared leaflet with details of groups relevant to his disability will be helpful. SCOPE and ASBAH, for example, have telephone helplines and counsellors and other organisations, such as SPOD and RELATE, offer counselling help. Many local authorities now produce resource booklets for disabled people in their area which the young person can obtain free of charge.

It is advisable for the counsellor to bear several factors in mind when preparing young people in this way. Very few authorities offer a counselling service. It does fall within the remit of general medical practices to fund counselling and some do employ a practice counsellor whose services are free to the client. These counsellors usually have a very long waiting list, are unable to undertake more than a brief course of counselling and may not have special knowledge of disability. Funding for counselling outside the practice setting is difficult to obtain.

Social Services will sometimes fund counselling, especially for clients attending day centres or residential establishments. However, this cannot be assumed. Some independent residential homes can offer payment of counsellor's fees.

Telephone helplines and counsellors who answer letters from clients can again offer limited services. A telephone call or letter may help in a crisis. Information can be helpful and leaflets offer information and resources. They may be able to offer referrals to a skilled counsellor but again, funding will be an issue.

The young person should realise that he may well have to pay counsellor's fees himself. Some people resent this, arguing that coun- selling should not have to be paid for. It needs to be pointed out that the counsellor is a professional person who has trained to earn her living in this way. If she is self-employed the fees she charges have to reflect her expenses in, for example, premises rental, telephone bills, insurance and taxes as well as paying the usual bills. Paying for counselling can be presented as true equality because the disabled person is treated in exactly the same way as able-bodied people in this respect.

It may be appropriate at this point to discuss one aspect of some children's perception of life as an able-bodied person. Many children who are disabled, as well as some adults, find it difficult to comprehend that a person who can walk or talk, for example, can have real and painful emotional problems. Nothing, they feel, can ever be as bad as having to contend with disability.

A man with cerebral palsy, a wheelchair user with difficult speech, was in his second year of a counselling course. He was asked what he found most difficult about being the only student with a disability. He replied, 'It was fighting my conviction that I was the only one with real problems. In our support group I would listen to other students talking about their difficulties in life, see their tears and anger and – all the time – say to myself, they're acting, this isn't real. No-one can have problems like mine. Now, after two years, I have finally won the battle and can recognise that able-bodied doesn't equal no problems. That has been more difficult for me than any other part of the course.'

It is probably too late to begin to teach a child who is leaving school that no man is an island when it comes to emotional pain. If he does think this it may prompt the counsellor, as it did those who heard the student, to introduce to teachers the idea of sharing with children that they too have their problems, difficult feelings and bad days. Obviously this should not be done in the way of Doc. Daneeka in the book *Catch 22* who greeted every patient's story with the response 'How do you think *I* feel!'

Maintaining contact

Some young people who have had counselling support and have formed a good relationship with the counsellor will ask for contact to be maintained. It is a tempting suggestion. Most counsellors would feel flattered at such an expression of confidence in their skills. It is neither a practical nor a desirable proposition and should not be considered except in exceptional circumstances. If the Health or Social Services have referred the client and wish counselling to continue it should be on a professional basis. The counsellor as well as the client should feel that continued counselling is appropriate. Otherwise it is all too easy for the counsellor to find herself attempting to visit several people on a voluntary basis, outside working hours and with clients who are becoming more and more dependent.

Few young people with special needs will leave school or college to live in an ideal environment. Many will have a difficult struggle to achieve real independence in the control of their own lives. Many will find life as hard and as frustrating as some of their able peers. Those who have had skilled counselling in childhood and as they grow up will have had the opportunity to begin to understand how to resolve their problems. They will know of the value of counselling and how to ask for it. Hopefully their demands will be met should they need counselling in the future.

Useful Organisations

The following list is a selection of organisations and groups connected with children, disability and counselling. It is by no means exhaustive. The books *Directory for the Disabled* (see Reading List) and *A Practical Guide for Disabled People*, produced by the Department of Health, are indispensable resources for any information not included here.

ACE (Aids to Communication in Education)
Ormerod School
Waynflete Road
Headington
Oxford OX3 8DD
Tel: 01865 63508

Association for Spina Bifida and Hydrocephalus (ASBAH)
ASBAH House
42 Park Road
Peterborough
Cambridgeshire PE1 2UQ
Tel: 01733 555988
Fax: 01733 555985

Blissymbolics Communication Resource Centre
Room Q
104 Queenswood
Cardiff Institute of Higher Education
Cyncoed Centre
Cardiff CF2 6YD
Tel: 01222 757826

British Association for Counselling
1 Regent Place
Rugby
Warwickshire CV21 2PJ
Tel: information –
01788 578328
administration –
01788 550899

British Epilepsy Association
Anstey House
40 Hanover Square
Leeds LS3 1BE
Tel: 0113 243 9393
Fax: 0113 242 8804
Helpline: 0800 309030

Brook Advisory Centre
National Office
165 Grays Inn Road
London WC1X 8UD
Helpline: 0171 713 9000
Computerised 24 hour helpline:
    0171 617 8000
Fax: 0171 833 8181

Carers National Association
20–25 Glasshouse Yard
London EC1A 4JS
Tel: 0171 490 8818
Carers line: 0171 490 8898
Fax: 0171 490 8824

Childline
Freepost 1111, London N1
Tel: 0800 1111
Minicom (2–9pm only):
    0800 400222

**Children's Head Injury Trust
    (CHIT)**
c/o Neurosurgery
The Radcliffe Infirmary
Oxford OX2 6RE
Tel: 01865 224786

Cystic Fibrosis Trust
Alexandra House
5 Blyth Road
Bromley
Kent BR1 3RS
Tel: 0181 464 7211
Fax: 0181 313 0472

Down's Syndrome Association
155 Mitcham Road
London SW17 9PG
Tel: 0181 682 4001
Fax: 0181 682 4012

Family Planning Association
27–35 Mortimer Street
London W1N 7RJ
Tel: 0171 837 5432
Fax: 0171 837 3026

**Makaton Vocabulary
    Development Project**
31 Firwood Drive
Camberley
Surrey GU15 3DQ
Tel: 01276 61390
Fax: 01276 681368

**MENCAP (Royal Society for
    Mentally Handicapped
    Children)**
123 Golden Lane
London EC1Y 0RT
Tel: 0171 454 0454
Fax: 0171 608 3254

Muscular Dystrophy Group of
  Great Britain and Northern
  Ireland
7–11 Prescott Place
London SW4 6BS
Tel: 0171 720 8055
Fax: 0171 498 0670

NASPCS (National Society of
  Incontinent and Stoma
  Children)
51 Anderson Drive
Valley View Park
Darvel
Ayrshire KA17 0DE
Tel: 01560 322024

National Deaf Childrens' Society
National Office
15 Dufferin Street
London EC1Y 8PD
Tel/textphone: 0171 250 0123
Helpline: 0800 252380
    Mon–Fri (1–5pm)
Fax: 0171 251 5020

National Society for Epilepsy
Chalfont Centre
Chalfont St Peter
Gerrards Cross
Bucks SL99 0RJ
Tel: 01494 873991
Fax: 01494 871927

PHAB (Physically Handicapped
  and Able-Bodied)
12–14 London Road
Croydon CR0 2TA
Tel: 0181 667 9443
Fax: 0181 681 1399

RADAR (The Royal Association
  for Disability and
  Rehabilitation)
12 City Forum
250 City Road
London EC1V 8AF
Tel: 0171 250 3222
Textphone: 0171 250 4119
Fax: 0171 250 0212

RNIB (Royal National Institute
  for the Blind)
224 Great Portland Street
London W1N 6AA
Tel: 0171 388 1266
Fax: 0171 388 2034

RNID (The Royal National
  Institute for Deaf People)
19–23 Featherstone Street
London EC1Y 8SL
Tel: 0171 296 8000
Textphone: 0171 296 8001
Fax: 0171 296 8199

SCOPE
12 Park Crescent
London W1N 4EQ
Tel: 0171 636 5020
Helpline: 0800 626216
Fax: 0171 436 2501

Spinal Injuries Association
76 St James's Lane
London N10 3DF
Tel: 0181 444 2121
Counselling line: 0181 883 4296
Fax: 0181 883 4926

SPOD (The Association to Aid
    the Sexual and Personal
    Relationships of Disabled
    People)
286 Camden Road
London N7 0BJ
Tel: 0171 607 8851

The Wolfson Childrens'
    Assessment Centre
Mecklenberg Square
London WC1
Tel: 0171 837 7618

Reading List

Reference

Gill Brearley and Peter Birchley (1994) *Counselling in Disability and Illness*, 2nd edn. Masby (Times Mirror International Publishers), London.

Accounts of childhood and disability

Reading biography and autobiography can increase awareness and give insight into how some people experience disability. Accounts of encounters with a wide variety of professional helpers are often revealing. The books listed are a small selection from a wide range on the market.

Patricia Collins (1981) *A Mother's Story*. Piatkus Books, London.
   The mother of a severely cerebral palsied child gives an account of her struggle to accept her daughter.

Rosemary Crossley and Anne McDonald (1982) *Annie's Coming Out*. Penguin Books, Harmondsworth.
   An account of the discovery and rescue of a highly intelligent and profoundly physically disabled child in an Australian hospital for the severely retarded, written by the young woman and her teacher.

Anne Deveson (1992) *Tell Me I'm Here*. Penguin Books, Harmondsworth.
   A biography by the mother of an autistic son.

Paddy Doyle (1988) *The God Squad*. Corgi Edition, London.
The harrowing autobiography of an institutionalised disabled child in the 1940s.

Bronwyn Hocking (1990) *Little Boy Lost*. Bloomsbury Publishing, London.
The mother of an autistic son whose comments on the agencies involved are enlightening.

Christopher Nolan (1987) *Under the Eye of the Clock*. Pan Books, London.
An autobiographical novel written by a non-verbally communicating young man very severely disabled with cerebral palsy.

Elisabeth Ward (1986) *Timbo: A Struggle for Survival*. Sidgewick and Jackson, London.
A book about the life and death of her son by the founder of the British Kidney Patient Association.

Nicholas Woolley and Sue Clayton (1989) *Just for William*. Penguin Books, Harmondsworth.
An account by the parents of their son with leukaemia.

Counselling and children

Virginia Axline (1964) *Dibs: In Search of Self*. Pelican Books, Harmondsworth.
Classic, definitive study of play therapy with an emotionally damaged child.

Mary McCracken (1974) *A Circle of Children*. Sphere Books, London.
An experience of group work with severely emotionally disturbed children.

Kathy Robinson (1991) *Children of Silence*. Penguin Books, London.
An account by their mother of her two deaf daughters, with information about the acquisition of language.

Russ Rymer (1993) *Genie*. Michael Joseph, London.
A narrative and an exposition regarding an abused and sensorily deprived child and the acquisition of language.

Sex education and information

Hilary Brown and Ann Craft (1992) *Working with the Unthinkable*. Family Planning Association, London. (Sex abuse and disability)

Ann Darnbrough and Derek Kinrade *The Sex Directory*. Woodhead-Faulkner, Cambridge. (Updated regularly)

Robie H. Harris (1994) *Let's Talk About Sex*. Walker Books, London.

Peter Mayle (1993) *Where Did I Come From?* Pan Books, London.

Peter Mayle (1993) *What's Happening To Me Now?* Pan Books, London.

Gill Mullinar (1992) *Sex Education Dictionary*. LDA, Wisbech.

Sex Education Forum (1993) *Religion, Ethnicity & Sex Education*. National Children's Bureau, London.

Disability and children

Valerie Sinason (1993) *Understanding Your Handicapped Child*. Rosendale Press, London.
Written primarily for mothers but with some useful insights into disability.

Resources for information and advice

These publications are updated at intervals:

Department of Health *A Practical Guide for Disabled People.*

Ann Darnbrough and Derek Kinrade *Directory for the Disabled* and *The Sex Directory.* Woodhead Faulkner, Cambridge.

Glossary

Alternative communication The use of systems that enable a child with no or unintelligible speech to communicate.

Ataxia Damage to the cerebellum of the brain affecting coordination and balance.

Athetosis Damage to the basal ganglia of the brain causing uncoordinated and unwanted movement.

Augmentative communication The use of systems that support or clarify communication for children with difficult speech or impaired language.

Blissymbolics A non-verbal form of communication in which the user indicates pictograms and concept-based symbols to access a complete language.

Body image A person's perception of his physical appearance and attributes that affect his behaviour and relationships.

Cerebral palsy A group of conditions caused by brain damage before, during or immediately after birth. Ataxia, athetosis and/or spasticity may be accompanied by sensory impairment and/or learning difficulties.

Client One who asks for, and receives, counselling.

Conditioned response A pattern of behaviour developed as a result of external demands.

Confidentiality The privacy of the client's disclosures within the counselling relationship.

Congruence A counselling skill in which the counsellor is aware of her own feelings in the counselling relationship and shares these with the client when this is appropriate.

Contract (counselling) An agreement between counsellor and client (or counsellor and supervisor) concerning confidentiality, boundaries, time and duration of sessions and the expectations of both persons regarding the counselling process.

Counselling   The use of skills and techniques that enable a client to recognise his problems and discover and implement his own resolutions.

Cystic fibrosis   A congenital illness causing thickened and sticky mucous secretions. This results in breathing and digestive impairment and early death.

Denial   A conscious or subconscious refusal or inability to recognise and/or acknowledge a painful fact.

Duchenne's muscular dystrophy   A genetically linked condition affecting boys which results in increasing muscular weakness and early death.

Empathy   The ability to share another's feelings and to experience the world as he perceives it.

Fantasy   A person's interpretation of what he perceives as reality, based on his own assumptions.

Learning difficulties   Specific or global impairment resulting in delayed, slow or incomplete learning.

Makaton   Hand signs derived from British Sign Language providing a simple form of communication.

Mayer-Johnson Picture Communication   An extensive vocabulary system of pictorial line drawings.

Rebus symbols   A communication system utilising stylised pictorial line drawings.

Reflecting   The counselling skill of repeating to a client in his own words or an equivalent form, a thought or feeling he has expressed.

Repression   Relegating to the unconscious, painful or unacceptable feelings and/or experiences.

Resolution   A strategy or course of action that enables the client to live a life he finds acceptable with a problem that may be intractable.

Role play   Interaction with another person or group of people where each assumes another persona or enacts a situation that has or might occur. Role play explores emotions and offers the opportunity to experiment with strategies for behaviour in a safe environment.

Spasticity   Damage to the cortex of the brain resulting in stiffness of muscles.

Special needs (children with)   Disability, impairment or disabling illness resulting in altered lifestyle, reduced expectations, learning difficulties and/or reduced life expectancy.

Strategy   A considered course of action to achieve a desired result.

Supervisor (in counselling)   A colleague with counselling skills with whom the counsellor can assess and evaluate her work with clients and explore and resolve her own feelings in a counselling relationship.

Index